Sweden's Welfare State

Can the Bumblebee Keep Flying?

Subhash Thakur
Michael Keen
Balázs Horváth
Valerie Cerra

International Monetary Fund
Washington, D.C.

Production: IMF Multimedia Services Division
Cover Design: Sanaa Elaroussi
Figures: Julio R. Prego
Typesetting: Alicia Etchebarne-Bourdin

Cataloging-in-Publication Data

Sweden's welfare state: can the bumblebee keep flying? / Subhash Thakur . . . [et al].—
[Washington, D.C.]: International Monetary Fund, [2003].

p. cm.

Includes bibliographical references.
ISBN 1-58906-158-6

1. Welfare state. 2. Sweden—Economic policy. 3. Sweden—Economic conditions.
4. Labor market—Sweden. I. Thakur, Subhash Madhav, 1946– II. International Monetary
Fund.

HC375.S83   2003

Price: $23.50

Please send orders to:
International Monetary Fund, Publication Services
700 19th Street, N.W., Washington, D.C. 20431, U.S.A.
Tel.: (202) 623-7430   Telefax: (202) 623-7201
E-mail: publications@imf.org
Internet: http://www.imf.org

recycled paper

. . . Think of a bumblebee. With its overly heavy body and little wings, supposedly it should not be able to fly—but it does. Every summer it comes back and makes the seemingly impossible possible en route from a forget-me-not to a daisy. This is how so-called analysts view the Swedish economy. We "defy gravity." We have high taxes and a large public sector, and yet, Sweden reaches new heights. We are still flying, so well that many envy us for it today.

— Prime Minister Göran Persson

Opening address on March 10, 2000 to the Extra Party Congress of the Social Democratic Party in Stockholm.

Contents

Tables

The following symbols have been used throughout this volume:

...   to indicate that data are not available;

—   to indicate that the figure is zero or less than half the final digit shown, or that the item does not exist;

–   between years or months (e.g., 2001–02 or January–June) to indicate the years or months covered, including the beginning and ending years or months;

/   between years (e.g., 2001/02) to indicate a fiscal (financial) year.

"Billion" means a thousand million.

Minor discrepancies between constituent figures and totals are due to rounding.

The term "country," as used in this paper, does not in all cases refer to a territorial entity that is a state as understood by international law and practice; the term also covers some territorial entities that are not states, but for which statistical data are maintained and provided internationally on a separate and independent basis.

Foreword

A key issue facing the world economy in the new century is the need to re-fashion a proper role for the state in economic affairs. The debate over the economic role of the state in the advanced industrial countries is a long-running one, and its centrality is manifest in the contrasting—and often passionately held—viewpoints on the appropriate role and limits of the welfare state.

This debate has come into sharper focus in recent years as these economies have tried to adjust to the powerful forces of rapid globalization of economic activity and the unavoidable aging of populations. Indeed, the issue at the heart of this debate—how to find the right balance between the imperatives of economic efficiency and those of economic and social equity—is increasingly a focus of the International Monetary Fund's surveillance of its members' economic policies.

In this context, the experience of Sweden is of particular interest. I hope that this study of the challenges facing the Swedish welfare state will prove instructive in the context of the wider global discourse on this important topic.

Anne O. Krueger
First Deputy Managing Director
International Monetary Fund

Preface

Sweden has long been viewed as epitomizing a particular approach to economic and social policy. To its critics, the Swedish welfare state is marked by excessive government intervention and attendant inefficiencies that impede the economy's ability to respond to shocks and impair its long-term growth performance. To its advocates, it is a social system building on a strong consensus favoring extensive intervention to ensure a high quality of life for all Swedish citizens—it is the bumblebee that somehow manages to fly. Just as important as assessing the past achievements and shortcomings of the Swedish welfare state, however, is the task of preparing for what lies ahead. Increasing internationalization of economic activity, combined with demographic pressures, seem likely to change the context within which Sweden must pursue its economic and social goals.

Through its continual surveillance of its members' economic policies, centered on an annual visit and assessment by staff, the International Monetary Fund has observed the workings of the Swedish welfare state for many years. It has offered its own advice, and sought to distill lessons for others. This book continues that process. It grew out of a visit to Stockholm in June 2001 by a mission headed by Subhash Thakur and comprising Balázs Horváth and Valerie Cerra (all of the European I Department) and Michael Keen (of the Fiscal Affairs Department).

This is an especially opportune moment to take stock of the achievements and prospects for the Swedish welfare state. The difficulties of the early 1990s have receded into the past, and the reforms adopted in their wake have been in place long enough to afford a considered assessment. And now the challenges of the new century loom. How Sweden responds to these is important not only to the Swedes themselves, but as a potentially valuable lesson to others. We hope that this book will help to inform what seems certain to prove a long and lively debate, with a resonance far beyond Sweden.

Michael Deppler
Director, European I Department

Teresa Ter-Minassian
Director, Fiscal Affairs Department

Acknowledgments

This book is the product of much hard work by other people. Among the staff of the IMF whom the authors would particularly like to thank are Richard Hemming, Robert Ford, C. Maxwell Watson, Eivind Tandberg, and Kornélia Krajnyák. Participants in seminars at the IMF and the Swedish Ministry of Finance, Erik S. Weisman, Vijay L. Kelkar, R.A. Jayatissa, and other members of the IMF's Executive Board have also provided useful comments. We have also benefited greatly from discussions at the Confederation of Swedish Enterprise, the Institute for International Economic Studies, Uppsala University, the Ministry of Finance, the Ministry of Industry and Labor, the Riksbank, the Office of Labor Market Program Evaluation, the Government of Uppsala, the Swedish Association of Local Authorities, and the Swedish Confederation of Trade Unions. The authors would like to thank Jonas Agell, Dan Andersson, Krister Andersson, Paul Armknecht, Sören Blomquist, Robert Boije, Per-Olof Edin, Johan Gull, John Hassler, Anders Kristoffersson, Assar Lindbeck, Thomas Lindh, Lars-Erik Lindholm, Michael Lundholm, Nils Mårtensson, Henry Ohlsson, Mats Persson, Jan Södersten, Lars Svensson, Gunnar Tersman, and Judit Weibull for useful comments and suggestions. We are grateful for assistance from Joy Rivera and Janet Shelley, and to Richard Phillips for research assistance. Sean M. Culhane of the IMF's External Relations Department edited the manuscript, and James McEuen of the External Relations Department copyedited it and coordinated its production and publication. The views expressed, however, are the sole responsibility of the authors, as are any remaining errors.

Subhash Thakur
Michael Keen
Balázs Horváth
Valerie Cerra

Abbreviations

AECT	Average effective corporate tax rate
ALMP	Active labor market program
EU	European Union
GDP	Gross domestic product
ICT	Information and communication technology
LO	Swedish Confederation of Trade Unions
MEB	Marginal excess burden of taxation
MECT	Marginal effective corporate tax rate
MEST	Marginal effective personal savings tax rate
MELT	Marginal effective labor income tax rate
MEPT	Marginal effective personal income tax rate
OECD	Organization for Economic Cooperation and Development
PAYG	Pay-as-you-go
PPP	Purchasing power parity
SKr	Swedish krona
SAF	Confederation of Swedish Employees
TFP	Total factor productivity
UN	United Nations
UNDP	UN Development Program
VAT	Value-added tax

1 Introduction and Overview

Sweden has long been regarded as epitomizing the modern welfare state. In fact, the "welfare states" of different countries differ in quite fundamental ways.[1] That in Sweden—naturally if somewhat imprecisely referred to as the "Swedish model"—is marked by the use of big, centralized institutions and large-scale transfers, commonly provided on a universal basis (rather than being income related) with a view to reducing inequality, alleviating poverty, and insuring against social risks. The key features of this policy regime, which employs both fiscal and nonfiscal measures, include:[2]

- An active and large state with a broad political mandate to intervene in the market process to secure equality of income and wealth distribution at a socially desired level;

- Highly ambitious social insurance arrangements covering an unusually wide array of risks and providing generous income replacement when they materialize;

- Relatively little use of means-tested benefits;

---

[1]Esping-Andersen (1990), for instance, identifies three types of welfare state: the "liberal," characterized by modest and largely means-tested benefits and strong stratification between welfare recipients and others (as in the United States); the "corporatist," concerned largely with preserving status rights and so providing, for example, benefits only loosely related to contributions (as in Germany); and the "social democratic," of which Sweden is the archetype, characterized by a considerable degree of universalism in benefits—provided at a level attractive even to the middle class—and committed to high employment levels both as a right and as a means to finance high benefits.

[2]Comprehensive accounts of the structure and history of the Swedish welfare state, from a variety of perspectives, can be found in Freeman and others (1997), Lachman and others (1995), Lindbeck (1997) and Lindbeck and others (1994), and OECD (2000).

- High levels of taxation and social security contributions, needed to sustain large-scale income transfers and sizable public consumption;

- Elaborate centralized institutions and structures aimed at facilitating effective cooperation between the private sector and a large, service-oriented public sector, with the latter responsible not only for the financing but also for the provision of most social services;

- Extensive regulatory and supervisory intervention (especially, but not only, in the labor market);

- Wages and working conditions set in a framework of centralized bargaining (involving employers and well-organized trade unions, but not directly the government, which participates only in its capacity as employer), aiming for full employment, stable labor income, and peaceful conflict resolution;

- Extensive public employment, concentrated in health care and education; and

- A relatively large share of publicly owned enterprises.

The Swedish model has consistently enjoyed solid support from all sections of Swedish society. This support seems to stem both from altruism and self-interest. The former seems evident, for example, in the relative generosity of Sweden's foreign aid program, while the latter is suggested by the pattern of survey responses. There are quite large differences in attitudes, for example, between private and public sector employees, with high-level public employees in Sweden showing more support for the welfare state than do high-level private sector employees. More generally—and not surprisingly—groups with a stronger market position, whether along a gender or class dimension, show weaker support for state intervention. At the other end, the unemployed—the group with the weakest market position—display the strongest support for state intervention. Indeed, similar patterns are repeated throughout the advanced economies, regardless of the nature and extent of welfare provisions.[3]

The welfare state in Sweden has many impressive achievements. Sweden's quality of life, public health, and educational attainment indicators are among the best in the world.[4] The country is politically stable, with high employment

---

[3]See, for instance, Svallfors (2002) and Boeri, Börsch-Supan, and Tabellini (2001).

[4]These aspects are critical in assessing economic performance. Nordhaus (2002) estimates, for instance, that improvement in health indicators over the past century may have raised welfare by an amount approximately equal to the increase in measured real consumption.

and participation rates and remarkably low levels of labor conflict. A high level of economic and gender equality, as well as substantial public support for the creation and preservation of human capital—both key features of the Swedish model—give rise to dynamic advantages that can offset any static efficiency losses arising from the higher public intervention in market processes. These dynamic advantages arise from, among other things: coverage against a wide array of risks not insurable in private markets (not least the risk of being born to poor or less-educated parents); greater use of talent resulting from higher female participation rates and the effective incorporation of minorities and immigrants into the labor market; greater ability to take risks owing to the presence of a strong social safety net; and enhanced intergenerational mobility. A greater degree of public intervention also has the potential to correct additional market failures arising from imperfect competition, asymmetric information, and various externalities. Not least, the pursuit of equality domestically is matched by relatively generous support for developing countries, and a high degree of sensitivity to environmental issues.

But maintaining a very large welfare state may involve substantial economic costs. The tax burden needed to sustain the welfare state in Sweden is among the highest in the world. Owing to the international mobility of capital, the effective burden of this is likely to be heavily concentrated on labor income. As shown in Figure 1, the high levels of direct taxation and social security contributions make the tax wedge on labor almost the highest in the OECD countries. This, together with generous welfare provisions, creates strong disincentive effects on effective labor supply and a sizable black economy, variously estimated at between 5 and 19 percent of GDP.[5] The centralized institutions associated with the Swedish model lack flexibility, hampering efficient and timely adjustment to rapidly changing economic conditions. The compressed wage scale—a direct consequence of the centralized wage bargaining regime— may adversely affect work incentives at the high end of the skill distribution and is likely to discourage investment in human capital. Last, but not least, Lindbeck (1997) and several other participants in the academic debate on the Swedish model have argued that its excessive size was causally related to Sweden's relatively weak growth performance since the 1970s, reflected in a marked decline in its ranking by per capita GDP within the OECD.

While it is impossible to pin down the "optimal" size of the welfare state precisely—views on this will reasonably differ both in factual assessments of its ef-

---

[5]National Tax Board (2000) and the European Commission (2001) estimate the share of the black economy in Sweden at up to and equal to 7 percent, respectively; the higher estimate is by Schneider and Enste (2000).

Figure 1. Tax Wedge[1]

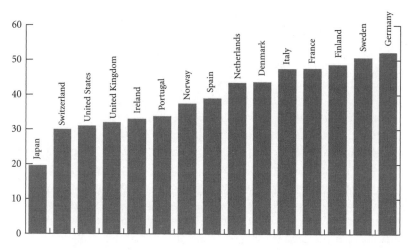

Source: OECD Online Statistics.
[1]Income tax plus employee and employer social security contributions in 1998. Single individual at income level of average production worker.

fects and in judging its ethical merit—government was generally agreed to have become too big by the late 1980s. The "overshooting" in the size of government of this period—a theme in Lindbeck (1997)—was amplified by demographic developments—Sweden's population was the oldest in the world during the 1980s—and was viewed as an underlying reason for the crisis in the early 1990s, whose proximate cause lay in external shocks and macroeconomic policy mistakes. Despite tax revenues exceeding 60 percent of GDP on the back of a strong cyclical upswing (Figure 2), high and volatile public consumption and transfers (Figure 3) led to large general government deficits (Figure 4) from 1991, and, with the onset of a crisis, to rapidly rising public debt, reaching three-quarters of GDP in the middle of the decade. The resulting surge in budgetary interest payments was coupled with a widespread loss of confidence in fiscal sustainability, precipitating the crisis of the early 1990s. The steady streamlining of government following the crisis was thus seen not just as a short-term correction of avoidable macroeconomic policy mistakes, but as a structural necessity. The large role played by government was also believed to hamper the flexibility of the economy to rebound from shocks. The subsequent less than complete recovery of lost output since the crisis period of the early 1990s, despite relatively rapid growth in the past few years, underscores the need for a renewed streamlining of the welfare state to maintain sustainable high growth.

Figure 2. General Government Revenues
(In percent of GDP)

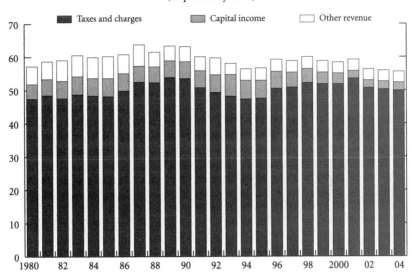

Whatever its past achievements and difficulties, the future seems certain to hold new challenges for the Swedish way of government. Globalization is changing the context in which the Swedish model operates by limiting its tax-based financing. In the past it was possible to maintain a drastically higher level of taxation to sustain a wide and all-encompassing social safety net and a pervasive role for the public sector in the economy, irrespective of what other countries did. But the fiscal basis for this strategy is being increasingly undermined. The scale and sensitivity of international capital flows make the base for taxing capital increasingly mobile. Rapid technological change, heightened regulatory and tax competition, and the increasing mobility of both commodities and labor pose further threats to budgetary revenues. Pressure can also be expected on the other side of the government's accounts, as the continued aging of the population increases spending needs. The government's ability to promote social objectives through regulatory measures is likely to be similarly constrained by greater private sector competition induced by globalization and deepening European integration.

The purpose of this short book is to review the prospects for the Swedish welfare state in the light of its past accomplishments. This is an important topic not only for the Swedes themselves but also for others who look to Swe-

Figure 3. General Government Expenditures
(In percent of GDP)

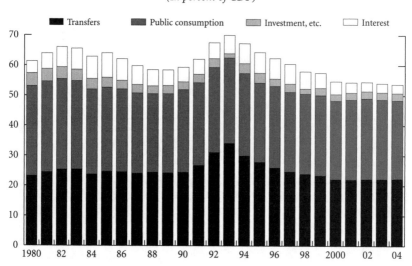

den for lessons of what government can, and cannot, do to foster social equality and growth. The Swedish economy has indeed been widely studied, and the welfare state more generally remains a subject of intense debate among both economists and the wider public.[6] This book draws on this extensive body of research to provide a relatively brief and accessible overview, and to assess the way ahead for Sweden.

The thrust of our argument is that it is both necessary and possible to streamline the Swedish model while preserving its key elements. Such a modified welfare state can underpin Sweden's competitiveness by building on the economy's existing strengths: effective governance in the public sector; wide-ranging public support for human capital creation, including through broad and efficient provision of education and health care; maintenance of high employment; and solidaristic assistance for the less fortunate at home and abroad to preserve social peace. Sweden's advanced position in the high-technology sector may also provide scope for enhancing public sector efficiency. Significant further strides in deregulation and privatization of state-owned enterprises in competitive markets would boost this process, and could help support the continuation of key elements of the welfare state. Finally, streamlining

---

[6]See, for example, Atkinson (1995, 1999).

Figure 4. General Government Balance
(In percent of GDP)

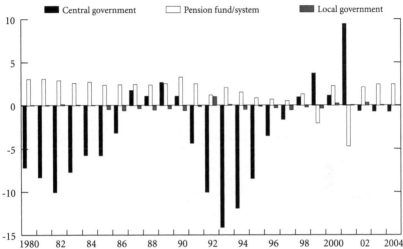

the Swedish model would involve a welcome reduction in the tax burden and in public spending, which should strengthen the fiscal position in the long run by raising employment, thus contributing to a broader tax base and reducing the need for budgetary transfers.

The book is structured as follows. Chapter 2 surveys the main elements of the Swedish welfare state. Chapters 3 and 4 explore the Swedish growth experience over recent decades and the extent to which it can be related, for better or worse, to the activities of government. Chapter 5 reviews labor market aspects, while the topic of Chapter 6 is investment and savings. Chapter 7 discusses redistribution, a central element of the Swedish model. Chapter 8 surveys various pressures on the welfare state, and Chapter 9 concludes with a short discussion on the future of the Swedish model and on lessons from the Swedish experience for other countries.

2   Main Elements of the Swedish Welfare State

This chapter provides context for the later discussion, describing key features of current arrangements in Sweden and of the development of the role of government over the past, critical decade.

Structure of Government, Social Welfare, and Taxation

The Swedish government comprises central and subnational levels, responsible for expenditures exceeding 54 percent of GDP (Table 1). The central government consists of ministries and central government agencies, and employed about 240,000 people in 1998. The ministries are small, most employing just a few hundred people. They are not concerned with details of administration, entrusting the implementation, management, and enforcement of government decisions and laws to about 250 central administrative agencies, and being constitutionally prohibited from interfering in their work. Subnational government comprises 21 regional and 289 local (municipal) governments. The primary responsibilities of county councils, which operate at a regional level, are health care and regional transport systems. Municipalities have a broad range of local responsibilities, including social services (childcare and programs for the elderly and families); primary, secondary, and adult education; land use planning and building permits; environmental and public health duties; technical services (water, sewerage, garbage collection); public emergency services; and some primary health care tasks.

Welfare services are highly developed and have decentralized delivery systems. Health and social care—seen as public sector responsibilities—are financed by county council revenues and central government grants, and delivered mainly by the county councils themselves. All residents in Sweden have

Table 1. General Government Expenditure
(In percent of GDP)

	2000	2001	2002	2003	2004
Transfers to households	19.0	19.0	19.1	19.2	19.0
Other transfers	3.2	3.0	3.0	3.0	3.3
Consumption expenditure	26.2	26.7	26.9	26.5	26.1
Central government and					
old-age pension system	7.5	7.5	7.6	7.4	7.3
Local government sector	18.6	19.1	19.3	19.1	18.9
Investments	2.2	2.3	2.4	2.4	2.4
Interest expenditure	4.2	3.4	3.0	3.0	2.9
Total expenditure	54.7	54.4	54.5	54.1	53.8
Exclusive of interest	50.5	51.0	51.5	51.1	50.9

Sources: Statistics Sweden; and Ministry of Finance.

access to health care, irrespective of whether they pay taxes or not. Medical, dental, and medicine charges above predefined and modest ceilings are borne by the public sector. National occupational injury insurance pays all health care costs for work-related accidents. The administration and delivery of most other welfare services are decentralized, involving local levels of government and also private entities.

Transfers to households are extensive: about 18 percent of GDP, compared with the OECD average of around 13 percent (Table 2). These transfers are also characterized by relatively limited reliance on means testing (on benefits, that is, whose extent is related to the recipients' current income from other sources). The principal transfers are summarized in Box 1. Most working people have unemployment insurance (tax financed, but administered by trade unions); the few without such coverage receive a lower benefit from the government. Extensive government programs for employment training, subsidized employment, job search assistance, and relocation assistance are available for the unemployed. A basic old age pension is payable as a citizen's right after age 65, topped up by a supplementary income-related pension.[7] The mother and father of a newborn are entitled to a total of 12 months of paid leave from work, with at least one month to be taken by the father. The parents also receive a flat, tax-free child allowance until the child reaches age 16. If the child continues education after that age, she is entitled to study allowances, as well as subsidized study loans for university studies. Means-tested benefits include housing allowances, highly subsidized day care and after-

---

[7]See Box 3 in Chapter 8 for more detail on the pension system and its recent reform.

Table 2. General Government Income Transfers, 2000
(In percent of GDP)

Australia	8.3
Austria	18.3
Belgium	14.4
Canada	10.9
Denmark	17.2
Finland	12.6
France	18.1
Germany	18.6
Greece	16.1
Ireland	9.7
Italy	17.3
Japan	15.7
Korea	3.3
Mexico (1995)	2.6
Netherlands	11.8
Norway	13.7
Portugal	12.5
Spain	12.4
Sweden	**18.3**
United Kingdom	13.1
United States	10.5
OECD average (excluding Mexico)	12.8

Source: OECD analytical database.

school care (if the parents are engaged in paid employment or in studies), together with financial and in-kind social assistance for those who cannot otherwise support themselves. Notable by its absence, however, is any general in-work income support measure akin to the U.S. Earned Income Tax Credit or the Working Families Tax Credit of the United Kingdom, both of which provide some add-on to take-home earnings that is higher the lower the level of before-tax earnings. Overall, about 7 percent of public social transfers are means tested; 29 percent are paid at a uniform rate to all recipients, and the rest is related to previous income. Reliance on means-tested benefits has traditionally been relatively low in Sweden. Esping-Anderson (1990) reports, for instance, that means-tested benefits in Sweden were only about 1.1 percent of social expenditure in 1980, compared with an average (over 18 developed economies) of about 6 percent.[8]

At around 52 percent, Sweden has the highest ratio of tax revenues to GDP of any OECD country. This fact is often noted, but there are important caveats

---

[8]Only Denmark had a (slightly) lower share of means testing. In the United States, at the other extreme, the corresponding figure was about 18 percent.

Box 1. Principal Transfers

Transfers in Sweden take the form of contingent benefits paid in an amount related to previous earnings, benefits paid in an amount related to contemporaneous income, or flat benefits. Most are taxable.

Earnings-Related Contingent Benefits

Unemployment benefit is paid for up to 300 days to those with an adequate employment history, at a rate of 80 percent of gross earnings (having been reduced, as with other benefits, to 75 percent in 1996), up to a maximum of SKr 680 per day for the first 100 days and of SKr 580 thereafter.

Sickness benefit is also paid at a replacement rate of 80 percent, up to a maximum of about 7.5 base amounts (a nominal sum defined in each year's budget law that forms the basis of most benefit calculations). Employers bear the cost for the first two weeks, and sometimes pay additional amounts. There is no duration limit.

Pensions are pay-as-you-go (PAYG), complemented by a funded component for those born after 1954 (see Box 3 in Chapter 8 for further details). The PAYG component aims to provide a replacement rate of two-thirds calculated using the best 15 years of earnings. Additional pension payments resulting from centralized bargaining agreements and from private funded schemes can add to this replacement rate.

Parental benefit allows parents to share 450 days of benefit at a replacement rate of 80 percent for 360 days, and with a guaranteed minimum for the remainder.

Child benefit, currently nontaxable, is paid for each child under 16, with a supplementary payment for the third and subsequent child.

Means-Tested Benefits

Social assistance is paid by local authorities to guarantee a minimum level of income. Rates are set by local authorities, but subject to a national minimum. Access is conditional not only on income but also on the level of assets.

Housing allowance is paid to those with children and to the young, at levels that vary with the number of children. The average withdrawal rate for families with children is 20 percent, and that for the young is 33 percent.

Childcare payments are subsidized for those in work, again at rates chosen by local authorities. Withdrawal rates are in the order of 5 to 7 percent, but expected to fall to 3 to 6 percent in 2002 with the introduction of capped payments for daycare, which will also weaken the link of this benefit to income levels.

Maintenance support is paid to those not receiving proper maintenance from an absent parent, with the latter then subject to reimburse the amounts paid in amounts related—with quite high marginal rates—to the debtor's income.

Student loans are provided to support studies in higher education, with repayment limited to 4 percent of income.

to be attached to international comparisons of the size of the public sector, implying that Sweden is not quite as much of an outlier in this respect as would appear from a simple comparison of the data:

- First, there are data comparability issues. Swedish revenue figures include the taxation of gross social transfers (significantly less heavily taxed in many other countries), raising measured revenue and expenditure levels by an estimated 4 percent of GDP in 2001.[9] Relatively high tax expenditures—revenue shortfalls from a hypothetical norm owing to tax exemptions, rebates, and preferential rates (estimated in Sweden at 5.7 percent of GDP in 2000)—also account in part for a relatively high measured tax burden.

- Second, welfare spending is driven not only by the generosity of transfer and social insurance payments, but also by the wage share and the dependency ratio.[10] Thus, the relatively early onset of aging of the Swedish population from the 1970s contributed to higher government spending compared with most OECD countries, whose populations had a significantly lower average age during the past three decades.

Nevertheless, it is striking that the Swedish tax ratio is not only far higher than the OECD average of 37.3 percent (which reflects the low ratios in the United States, Japan, Korea, and Mexico) but is also higher than the EU average of 42 percent.[11]

Around 40 percent of tax revenue is raised by income taxes, personal and corporate. The composition of revenues is shown in Table 3, while Table 4 compares some key direct tax rates in Sweden with those in the EU, Japan, and the United States; comparative rates of indirect taxation are given in

---

[9]In fact, the spring 2001 budget estimated that the effect of taxing gross social transfers on the tax ratio averaged between 5 and 6 percentage points of GDP during 1990–98.

[10]As noted by Atkinson (1995), the share of welfare spending (WS) in GDP can be written as:

$$\left(\frac{WS}{GDP}\right) \equiv \left(\frac{B}{w}\right)\left(\frac{wL}{GDP}\right)\left(\frac{R}{L}\right),$$

where B denotes the average benefit level, w the average wage, L the number of workers, and R the number of benefit recipients.

[11]Adema (1997) derives internationally comparable figures on the share of public social expenditure in GDP for 1993, controlling in particular for differences in direct taxes and social contributions paid on transfers, indirect taxes on consumption purchased out of net cash transfers, and tax breaks for social purposes on public and private social expenditure. Sweden still comes out at the top of the list of the eight OECD countries covered in the study, but the difference relative to the United States shrinks from 26 percentage points of GDP using unadjusted data to 15 percentage points, and becomes insignificant relative to Denmark, the other highly taxed OECD economy.

Table 3. Composition of Tax Revenues in Sweden, 1998
(In percent of GDP)

	Sweden	OECD[1]
Personal income tax	18.6	10.1
Corporate income tax	3.2	3.3
Employer's social security	10.0	5.8
Employee's social security	3.0	2.8
Taxes on payroll	3.9	0.4
VAT	7.2	6.9
Excises and other indirect taxes	3.7	4.2
Property	1.9	1.9
Other	4.4	2.3
Total	52.2	37.3

Sources: OECD (annual), *Revenue Statistics* (Paris).
[1]Unweighted average.

Chapter 8 (see Table 18). Like most other Nordic countries, Sweden has a "dual income tax" under which labor income is taxed at progressive rates, while capital income is taxed at a flat rate of 30 percent. Adoption of the dual income tax was the key structural innovation of the landmark tax reform of 1991, described in Box 2. The central rationale was the increasing difficulty of taxing capital income given the opportunity to evade tax by investing abroad and failing to declare the receipts (an issue pursued further in Chapter 8).[12] Labor income is taxed by both central and local government, the latter at a flat rate and the former applying only to incomes in excess of a relatively high threshold. The combined top marginal rate of tax on labor income is around 53 percent, and thus far exceeds the rate of tax on capital income. This creates significant difficulties—especially in connection with the self-employed and small businesses—from the need to enforce a distinction between the two kinds of income.

The logic of the dual income tax suggests that corporate income be taxed at the same rate as capital income, and dividends be exempt (since they are paid out at after-tax income). In fact, Sweden taxes corporations at the slightly lower rate of 28 percent, and dividends are not fully taxed.

Social security contributions are high—raising about one-quarter of all revenues—and levied mainly on the employer. The rate on earnings paid by employers is around 33 percent, while employees pay a further 7 percent. However, the government has embarked on a four-step plan of income tax reductions

[12]For detailed discussion of the rationale for and experience with the dual income tax, see Sørenson (1994) and Cnossen (2000).

Table 4. International Comparison of Tax Rates as at April 1, 2002
(In percent unless otherwise indicated)

	Taxes on Capital and Capital Income				Taxes on Labor Income (excluding social security)		
	Corporation tax[1]	Highest marginal rate on interest (dividends, if different)	Highest marginal wealth tax rate	Wealth tax threshold (in euros)[2]	Starting marginal rate (including surcharges)	Highest marginal rate (including surcharges)	Threshold[2] (in euros)
Austria	34	25	None (abolished 1994)		21	50	7,864[3]
Belgium	39 (40.2)	25	None		26	55	5,480
Denmark	30	59 (38.6)[4]	None		38.1[4]	47.6[4]	4,627[5]
Finland	29	29	0.9	185,000	24.5[6]	52.5[6]	11,500
France	33.33 (34.33)	25 (61[7])	1.8	720,000	7.5	52.75	4,121
Germany	25 (38.875)	48.5 (24.25)	None		19.96	48.5	7,235
Greece	37.5	20 (0)	None		15[7]	40.0	8,400[8]
Ireland	16[9]	44	None		20	42	7,600[5]
Italy	36[10]	27 (12.5)	None		18	45	6,312[11]
Japan	47.8	20 (35)	None		12.5	50	3,127

Luxembourg	22 (22.88)	42	0.5	40,000[12]	8	38.95	10,350[11]
Netherlands	34.5	25	None (abolished 2001)		32.35	52	15,331
Portugal	30 (33)	20	None		12	40	5,591[13]
Spain	35	48[7]	2.5	167,129	18	48	3,612
Sweden	28	30	1.5	134,477	28[14]	53[14]	1,506
United Kingdom	30[15]	40 (32.5[7])	None		10	40	3,045[11]
United States	35[15] (38.25[16])	42.15[16]	None		14.3[16]	42.15[16]	3,248

Sources: International Bureau of Fiscal Documentation, *European Tax Handbook 2000*; and Price Waterhouse, *Corporate Taxes 2002–2003* and *Individual Taxes 2002–2003*.

[1] Figures in parentheses include local and other surcharges.

[2] For a single person. Figures for Sweden and the United Kingdom use exchange rates as at October 1, 2001.

[3] Comprising a zero-rate band of €3,640 and a tax credit of €887.

[4] Assumes local income tax at the average marginal rate of 32.6 percent.

[5] Amount shown is threshold equivalent of a tax credit.

[6] For a resident of Helsinki.

[7] Not including a partial credit for underlying corporation tax.

[8] For an employee living on the mainland.

[9] To be reduced to 12.5 percent in 2003.

[10] To be reduced to 34 percent in 2003.

[11] For an employee.

[12] For bank deposits and debt claims, and including a basic allowance against the wealth tax. Other (and generally smaller) exemptions apply for other assets.

[13] Comprising a zero-rate band of €4,100 and a tax credit of €208.8.

[14] For a resident of Stockholm.

[15] This rate applies to the highest level of profits; to ensure that this is also the average rate at the highest profit levels, higher marginal rates apply at some lower levels of profit.

[16] Assuming state and local tax at 5 percent.

Box 2. Sweden's 1991 Tax Reform

The 1991 tax reform significantly broadened the tax base, markedly lowered the highest marginal income tax rates, eliminated various tax shelters, and—the main structural component—established the dual income tax.[1] This reform was designed to leave tax revenue unchanged and be close to neutral in terms of the overall distribution of net income, with the cuts in top marginal income tax rates offset by a new capital income taxation system—capital income tax revenue having been negative, with deductions exceeding receipts—and the elimination of tax loopholes and nonuniformities that had principally benefited the rich. The overall purpose was to enhance the efficiency and sustainability of the tax system through a massive shift of the tax burden from labor income to consumption and to individual capital income.

The magnitude of the shifts in the tax burden was quite exceptional, with pre-reform estimates of the negative impact on the budget of tax rate cuts and envisaged increases in transfers of around 6 percent of GDP. This was to be offset by other elements of the reform: over a third from the new system of taxing capital income, a third from the broadening of the base of the standard 23 percent VAT rate, and 15 percent from the elimination of loopholes and preferences on earned income. The remainder was to be covered by revenue gains generated by higher output stemming from improved incentives associated with the new tax system. In the event, these revenue gain projections proved to be overly optimistic, and the reform was underfinanced by about 4 percent of GDP.

Experience with the dual income tax is generally seen as broadly positive, the main difficulties being those associated with enforcing the distinction between capital and labor income given a difference in marginal tax rates of up to 20 percent. The reform unified the bewildering array of different tax rates on the returns from various assets, and eliminated loopholes related to differential tax shields available to private and public sector entities as well as the perverse incentives stemming from the possibility of claiming tax preferences on both personal assets and liabilities (making the purchase of real estate from borrowed funds a massive, low-risk source of net tax gains). Given the higher mobility of the tax base for capital than for labor income, and the Swedish model's continuing need for very high tax revenues, the dual income tax has proved to be a workable innovation, and one in which many other countries have taken much interest.

The tax reform was a systematic effort to overhaul the budgetary foundation of the Swedish model without reducing its size. It was implemented without much of a transition, and against the background of the deepest recession since the Great Depression (perhaps even adding to its severity). While its design undoubtedly had excellent elements and it might have fared better in a more tranquil macroeconomic environment, it alone was not—and could not have been—sufficient to avert the need for rolling back the overall level of taxation, and with it the size of the Swedish model, in subsequent years.

---

[1]Agell, Englund, and Södersten (1995) provide a comprehensive analysis and assessment.

(each costing about 0.6 percent of GDP) intended to compensate for the employees' contribution, the final step of which remains to be enacted in 2003.[13]

Value-added tax (VAT) is charged at a standard rate of 25 percent, the highest not only in the EU (along with Denmark) but in the world. It collects, however, only 7.2 percent of GDP (see Table 3), reflecting the application of a reduced rate of 12 percent to foods, passenger transport, hotels, and camping. The effective average rate of VAT—revenues relative to all private consumption—is thus only in the order of 17 percent. Revenue from excises—levied at high rates (as discussed in Chapter 8)—and property are broadly in line with OECD and EU averages, and relatively less important as a source of revenue.

Past Developments in Fiscal Aspects of the Swedish Model

The dramatic increase in the size of the Swedish government was halted following the crisis of the early 1990s, giving way to a steady retrenchment (see Figure 5).[14]

Expenditures surged during 1970–82, followed by an unsustainable squeeze, giving rise to temporary budget surpluses and another, even larger run-up during 1989–93. The expenditure ratio reached 70 percent of GDP in 1993 (26 percentage points higher than in 1970), but has been on a declining trend since then, projected to fall to 53 percent of GDP in 2004. Revenues peaked in 1989 at 63.7 percent of GDP, 15.4 percentage points higher than in 1970, and—with a variance just a third of that of expenditures—were much less volatile. The trend lines for expenditures and revenues suggest that a marked reversal in the size of government has begun and that a sustained surplus is emerging. Notably, the swing in expenditures was substantially more pronounced over the past decades than that in revenues. However, official projections through 2004 indicate that the momentum for further reductions in the size of government from its current high level may be flagging.

---

[13]The essence of the compensation scheme is as follows. Let Y denote income and e the employee's social security contribution rate. Given $T(.)$, the income tax schedule, and with no compensation, the income tax plus social security contribution liability is $L = T(Y - eY) + eY$. The compensation takes the form of an income tax credit for a proportion α of the social security payment, allowing only the uncredited portion $1 - \alpha$ as a deduction. Thus, total liability is $L^* = T[Y - (1 - \alpha)eY] + (1 - \alpha)eY$, with α being increased in four steps from 0 to 1.

[14]Data underlying the spring 2001 budget are based on the European System of Accounts (ESA-95) standard from 1980. While data for the 1970s are based on an earlier definition, they were appended without a visible break.

Figure 5. General Government Revenues and Expenditures
(In percent of GDP)

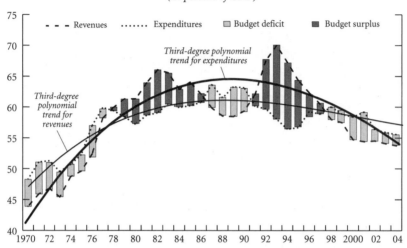

One key lesson from the run-up in spending to the mid-1990s, and its partial reversal since, is that expenditure control is central to sound public finance in Sweden. During the past three decades, large expenditure increases always preceded the emergence of sustained and substantial deficits. At the beginning of both deficit periods, revenues actually fell while expenditures raced ahead toward an unsustainable local peak. As a result, the average deficit, at 4.9 percent of GDP, was much larger than the average surplus (3.5 percent of GDP). Moreover, expenditure levels in excess of 60 percent of GDP were invariably associated with large deficits (concurrently or with a lag, following a short period of surpluses). Accounting for cyclical factors does not alter the conclusion that the fiscal balance deteriorated during the 1970s and 1980s. The key reason for this was a steady upward drift in expenditures stemming from a political consensus in favor of extending welfare arrangements, and strong demographic effects amplifying the tendency—observed throughout the OECD—of rising per capita incomes to be associated with an increase in the size of government.

General government expenditures have been effectively constrained by medium-term fiscal rules since 1997. These rules—which, together with an inflation target of 2 percent, form the core of macro policy in Sweden—comprise three elements:[15]

---

[15]For a detailed assessment of Sweden's fiscal strategy, see Schimmelpfennig (2002).

- a target of 2 percent of GDP for the general government structural surplus;

- ceilings on central government nominal expenditures (on noninterest expenditure plus spending on old age pensions outside the state budget), set on a rolling basis three years ahead; and

- a balanced budget requirement for local governments, stipulating a reversal of any deficits on current spending within two years.

The nominal expenditure ceilings set in 2001 and reconfirmed in the 2002 spring budget imply that the share of these expenditures will continue to decline (see Figure 6). Local governments have incurred deficits through the late 1990s, but the municipality sector as a whole has shown a small surplus since 2000 (although about 40 percent of municipalities still had a deficit). County councils continue to record considerable deficits, but the pension system has essentially always been in surplus, as shown earlier in Figure 4.[16]

Public consumption and transfers—accounting for 27 and 25 percent of GDP on average, respectively—both peaked in the early 1990s (see Figure 3). However, while the level of transfers is about the same now as it was in the early 1980s, enhanced expenditure control helped reduce public consumption by about 4 percentage points of GDP during the same period. The composition of transfers has shifted dramatically since the crisis period. Transfers to business were cut by 7 percentage points of GDP to a quarter of their 1993 level, while those to households were reduced by 5 percentage points, returning them to around their 1980 level. The share of transfers abroad in GDP has marginally grown. With the rapid rise in public debt during the early 1990s, interest payments increased sharply. Once the public debt situation improved—with the debt ratio back down to around 54 percent of GDP by 2000—the share of interest payments in GDP began to moderate, dropping to less than half of its mid-1990s peak by 2001.

The role played by government in the delivery of services, in regulation, and in managing public enterprises has also been redefined during the crisis-induced reforms.[17] The transparency of central government operations in the enterprise sector was greatly enhanced by moving the government's commercial activities to "arm's length" and clearly separating these activities from the exer-

---

[16]The large pension system deficits in 1999 and 2001 resulted from nonrecurring transfers to central government as part of the reform of the pension system and boosted central government surpluses, with no effect on the general government balance.

[17]See Gustafsson and Svensson (1999), and Ministry of Finance (2000).

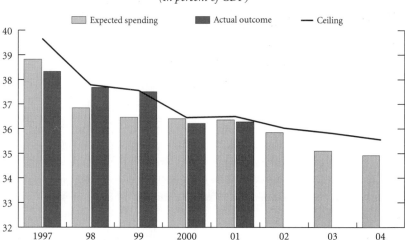

Figure 6. Central Government Expenditure Ceilings
(In percent of GDP)

cise of other government responsibilities. Large public monopolies (telecom, post office, energy company, forest management, and retail trade in alcohol and medicine) were corporatized and restructured to operate in a manner similar to private joint stock companies. The monopoly position of these publicly owned enterprises was reduced, their regulation strengthened, and competition with private entities cautiously encouraged. Given the lack of political consensus in favor of divesting public assets, however, only limited progress was made in privatizing state-owned enterprises. Indeed, Sweden still does not have a formal privatization program, even for state-owned enterprises in highly competitive sectors. Another important element in reforming central government was to redefine the roles of agencies, redistributing their responsibilities, and streamlining and focusing their operations to enhance their effectiveness and responsiveness. Government operations were also decentralized by delegating more decision-making rights to agencies from ministries, and from central to regional and municipal governments.

3 The Swedish Growth Experience

Sweden's growth performance over recent decades has been a matter of considerable interest and controversy, both within Sweden and more widely. There has been a long-running debate on the question of whether Sweden has suffered a relative decline in economic growth and living standards and, if so, the reasons for such a decline. Much of this debate has focused on the empirical question of the accurate measurement of Sweden's economic performance relative to that of other advanced economies and various technical issues germane to this question. This chapter addresses these issues and describes the wider experience of growth in Sweden more generally. This is an essential preliminary to approaching the other key issue in this debate, which is of special importance to the concerns of this book and is taken up in the chapter after this: whether this decline, if such there has been, can be attributed to interventions of the welfare state.

Has Swedish Growth Lagged Behind?

Between the middle of the nineteenth century and 1950, Sweden moved from being one of the poorest countries in Europe to one of its richest. Industrialization based on raw materials, an exceptionally high rate of labor productivity growth, and Swedish neutrality in the World Wars brought about a century of uninterrupted strong economic growth, boosting the country's relative per capita GDP position (Table 5).

Although Sweden's per capita income declined relative to the average of the 12 European countries over the subsequent 20 years, it still retained its high ranking through 1970. However, Lindbeck and others (1994) noted that Sweden's ranking among OECD countries fell from number 3 in 1970 to number

Table 5. Sweden's Relative GDP
(Per capita)[1]

1870	1913	1950
79.8	83.9	134.4

Source: Maddison (2001).
[1]At 1990 PPP dollars relative to the 12 largest European economies.

14 in 1991. Since this observation generated considerable debate, the data on which it was based are reproduced here for reference (Table 6).[18]

The apparently sharp decline in Sweden's ranking has been a subject of intense debate. Some scholars argue that measurement problems, sample period selection, and other factors give an appearance of relative decline, whereas Sweden's income has been, in fact, fairly stable in relative terms. Moreover, there may be reasons other than Sweden's welfare state—such as demography, catching up by others, and avoidable macroeconomic mistakes—that have led to any relative decline. This section discusses these various issues of interpretation and alternative explanations of the data.

The use of current exchange rates or arbitrary measurement intervals could produce misleading and volatile GDP comparisons. Periods of deteriorating terms of trade and of rampant inflation can contribute to an erosion of the exchange rate and a diminishing relative income position. Developments in the U.S. dollar-ECU or dollar-euro cross rates also affected the position of the Swedish krona at times, such as in the mid-1980s. Korpi (1996) used 1985 exchange rates to present Sweden's relative income over time. In 1985, the U.S. dollar was strong relative to the European Monetary System currencies, and the Swedish krona was tied to a basket with a disproportionate weight on the U.S. dollar. The use of a strong krona presented the level of Sweden's income favorably. Purchasing power parity (PPP) adjusted exchange rates are widely used in cross-country growth comparisons to help avoid this problem. However, some economists disfavor the PPP measure because it is based on an average OECD consumption basket that does not take into account goods and services provided by the government.

Sweden's initial high income position would suggest that a part of the decline in its relative income level reflects a convergence phenomenon. Countries with lower initial per capita income will tend to have higher growth rates as they "catch up" with the richer countries, through, among other factors, the

[18]Sweden's relative ranking in 1998 was 17.

Table 6. Sweden's Ranking in per Capita Income Between 1970 and 1991

1970 Rank		Index	1991 Rank		Index
1	Switzerland	145	1	United States	125
2	United States	141	2	Switzerland	122
3	Luxembourg	108	3	Luxembourg	120
3	**Sweden**	**108**	4	Germany	110
5	Germany	105	5	Canada	108
6	Canada	102	5	Japan	108
7	Netherlands	101	7	France	103
8	Denmark	100	8	Denmark	99
8	France	100	9	Belgium	98
10	Australia	99	10	Austria	97
11	New Zealand	98	10	Iceland	97
12	United Kingdom	93	12	Italy	95
13	Belgium	90	12	Norway	95
14	Austria	86	14	**Sweden**	**94**
15	Italy	85	15	Netherlands	93
16	Finland	82	16	Australia	91
17	Japan	80	17	Finland	90
18	Norway	77	18	United Kingdom	88
19	Iceland	75	19	New Zealand	78
20	Spain	64	20	Spain	72
21	Ireland	50	21	Ireland	65
22	Portugal	42	22	Portugal	52
23	Greece	41	23	Greece	44
24	Turkey	17	24	Turkey	20

Sources: OECD National Accounts; and Lindbeck and others (1994).

importation of technology. Although this factor need not imply a change in countries' per capita output rankings, it should force the levels to converge. Convergence would make it easier for small differences in other factors to significantly affect country rankings. Convergence implies that even if countries' rankings remain the same, there should be a decline over time in the relative income levels of the initially rich countries. Dowrick and Nguyen (1989) estimated that Sweden's smaller scope for catching up reduced growth by 0.8 percentage points during the period 1950–73 compared with the OECD average. Decomposing growth, they found that the rate of differential total factor productivity (TFP) growth was 0.79 percent per year in 1950–60, and –0.25 percent per year in 1973–85.

The choice of sample periods can have a decisive influence on the change in relative rankings of per capita income. The levels of output of a large group of fairly rich OECD countries are so close to each other that different states of the business cycle can produce volatile rankings among the countries. The

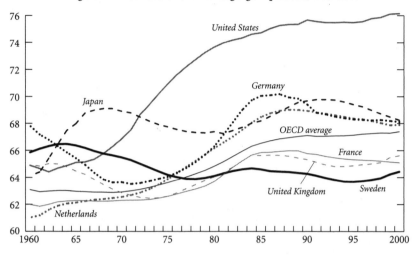

Figure 7. Sweden and OECD: Working-Age Population, 1960–2000

Sources: OECD; IMF, *World Economic Outlook*; and IMF staff calculations.

comparison of ranking in Lindbeck and others (1994) relies on the endpoints of 1970 and 1991. According to Korpi (1996), the high Swedish ranking in 1970 is based on a peak in economic activity, as growth was 5.6 percent in this year. Sweden drops to 14th place only in the final year of 1991, which was the beginning of a major recession. Korpi's presentation of 1973 and 1989 shows Sweden's position in a more favorable light because in 1973 Sweden suffered a relatively deep recession, while in 1989 it was in the midst of an unsustainable boom. Thus, the choice of the sample's endpoints can change substantially the conclusion about Sweden's relative decline.

The timing of the demographic transition is another important consideration. A higher share of the elderly reduces labor supply, and thus the level of output. In addition, it tends to imply a lower overall savings rate and differences in growth rates between countries. One of the reasons underlying Sweden's relative decline in the OECD's ranking by per capita GDP may be that the demographic shock of an aging population hit Sweden well before other countries. This was the consequence of the earlier rapid expansion, which was boosted by the relatively young population after World War II, which, unlike in other European countries, was not decimated by the war. Figure 7 shows that the ratio of working-age persons to the total population declined slightly over the four decades through 2000, while the percentage rose in an average of 24 OECD countries.

Figure 8. Sweden and OECD: GDP per Capita, 1960–2000
(1995 prices and PPP exchange rates)

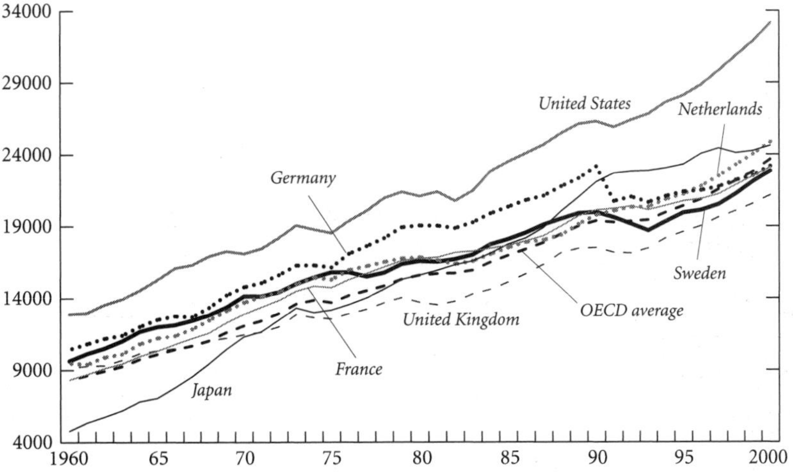

Sources: OECD; IMF *World Economic Outlook;* and IMF staff calculations.

Viewed over a longer span of years, Sweden seems to have slipped in the table of rankings of living standards as measured by per capita income. Figures 8 and 9 analyze the developments in Sweden's relative income position, taking into account several of these arguments. To avoid problems of sample period selection, the entire path of relative per capita output is shown. The effects of convergence can be viewed by comparing the paths of other initially rich countries and of Sweden. Figure 8 shows the path of per capita GDP in Sweden and 23 other OECD countries over the period 1960–2000 based on 1995 prices and PPP exchange rates. From the mid-1970s through around 1990, most countries experienced a slight slowdown in growth, but growth in countries took off again in the 1990s. Between 1960 and the mid-1970s, Sweden was in the top half of the countries in the sample, but its per capita income was fairly close to levels of many countries. Sweden's per capita income appears to have grown broadly in line with the bulk of countries concentrated in the center of the sample until 1990. In the early 1990s, Sweden's banking crisis and recession appear to have led to a permanently lower level of output, allowing a number of the countries to overtake Sweden in the GDP per capita rankings.

The slippage in Sweden's relative income reflects the convergence phenomenon. Figure 9 compares each country's GDP per capita to the average of the 24

Figure 9. Sweden and OECD: Relative GDP per Capita, 1960–2000[1]
(1995 prices and PPP exchange rates)

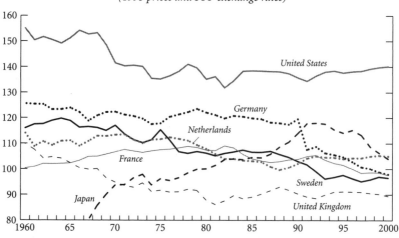

Sources: OECD; IMF, *World Economic Outlook;* and IMF staff calculations.
[1]Each country's GDP per capita is calculated as a percentage of the average of the 24 countries.
Turkey is included but not shown; its relative income was broadly stable between 25–30 percent.

countries, and shows that, with the exception of a few outliers, there has been a pattern of convergence in relative incomes in OECD countries. Sweden's relative income has trended down over the four decades, with most of the decline occurring in the mid-1970s and around 1990. The oil price shocks of the 1970s hit Sweden relatively hard, given its energy-intensive production structure (with heavy dependence, in particular, on forestry and pulp and automobile manufacture). Forestry, accounting for 40 percent of Swedish exports in the early 1970s, was particularly impaired by severe terms of trade shocks.

The deterioration in Sweden's relative position is corroborated by measures of output per working-age population. One alternative measure to output per capita that takes account of the differences in demographic structure across countries is output per employed person. However, employment rates vary with the business cycle, and long-term unemployment rates differ across countries. Output per employed person could be high due to either a high level of output or an exceptionally high unemployment rate. To avoid these problems, output per working-age person is used as an alternative income measure that adjusts for the demographic structure. To investigate the possibility that some of the value of production in a country represents income to foreigners, the comparison of gross national product (GNP), which includes net income flows to nonresidents, can be substituted for gross domestic product (GDP). Figure 10 compares these alternative measures of income. The top

Figure 10. Sweden and OECD: Income Measures
(1995 PPP)

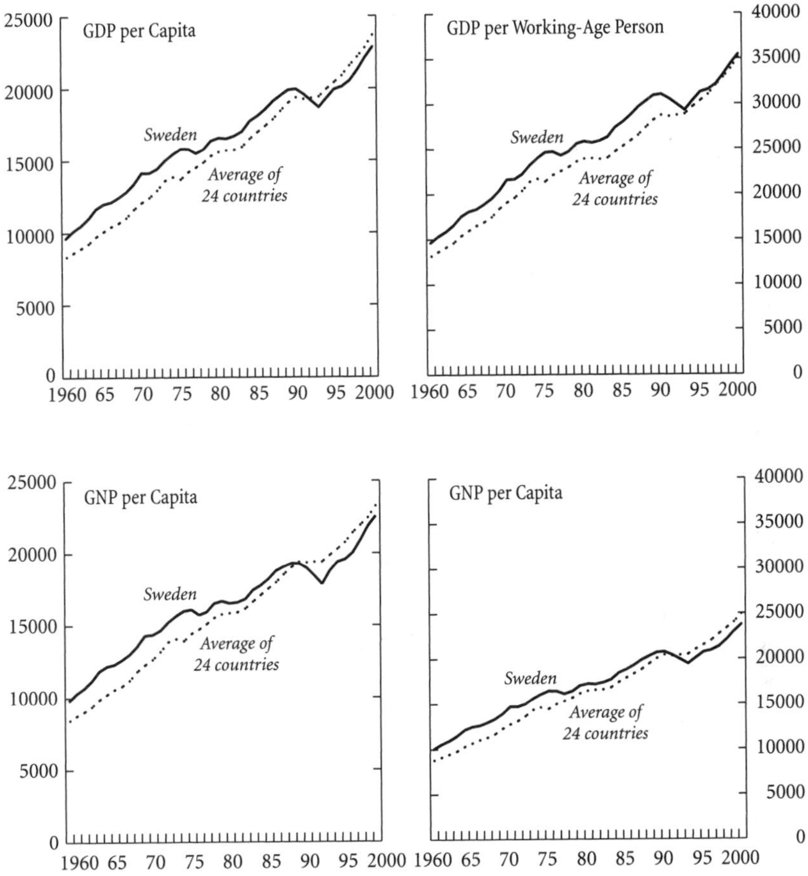

Source: OECD; IMF, *World Economic Outlook,* and IMF staff calculations.

(bottom) panels present GDP (GNP), while the left (right) panels divide the country's income by its total population (working-age population). All four measures show that Sweden maintained its relative position above the average until its severe recession in the early 1990s. From the early 1990s, Sweden's relative GDP and GNP per capita fell below the average of the 24 countries, whereas its relative GDP and GNP per working-age person fell to approximately the same level as the average. Sweden's position based on GDP is also somewhat superior to its position based on GNP. Figure 11 shows GDP per capita based on prices and PPP exchange rates from several different

Figure 11. Sweden and OECD: Income at Different PPP, 1960–2000

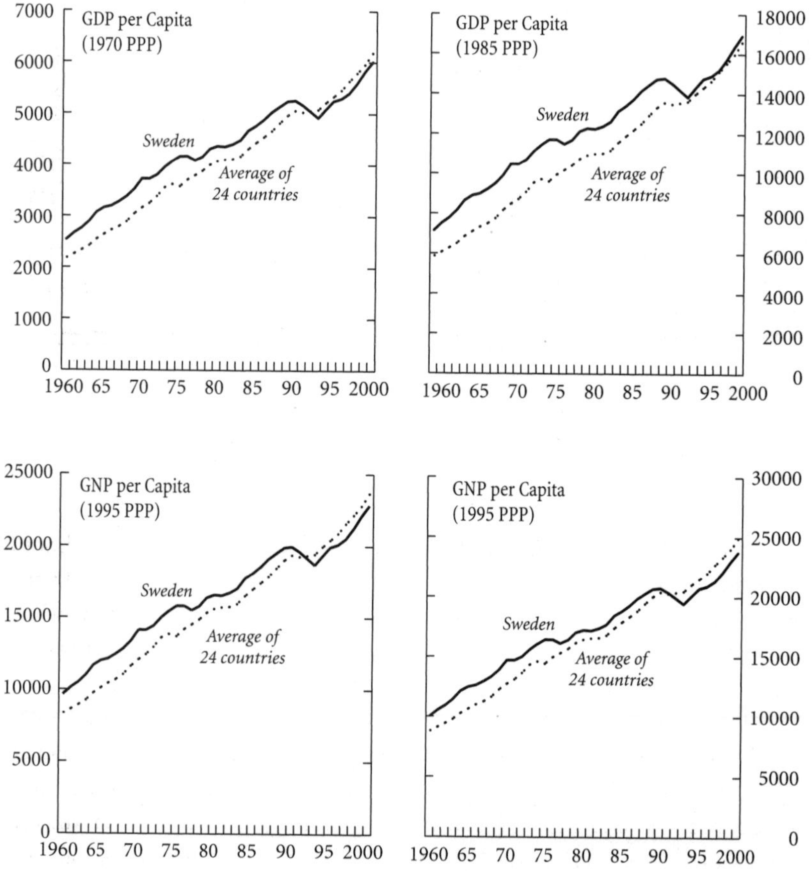

Sources: OECD; IMF, *World Economic Outlook,* and IMF staff calculations.

years. Sweden's relative GDP is broadly similar using 1970, 1995, and 1999 prices and exchange rates, but its relative position improves using 1985 as the base year.

It seems clear that macroeconomic policy errors leading to the crisis of the early 1990s played a key role in Sweden's relative slippage. The analysis above demonstrates that Sweden's relative GDP per capita declined over 1960–2000, with a significant relative deterioration in the early 1990s. Sweden made serious policy mistakes during 1974–92. It lagged other OECD countries in moving toward a low inflation environment and liberalizing capital markets by up

Figure 12. Probabilities of Permanent and Temporary Output Losses

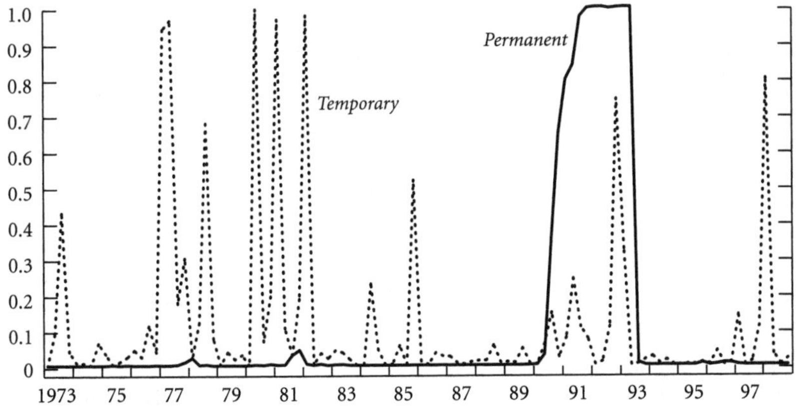

Source: IMF staff estimates.

to 12 years. The policy mistakes following Sweden's postliberalization boom contributed to a banking crisis and sharp recession in the early 1990s. In the latter half of the 1980s, Sweden maintained a fixed exchange rate regime while having high inflation and rapid credit expansion. High inflation and tax effects interacted to produce negative real interest rates. Sweden then began a tax reform without suitable expenditure side adjustment. Real interest rates and the fiscal deficit skyrocketed, asset markets collapsed, most major banks' capital base was virtually wiped out, and unemployment reached unprecedented levels. Public debt jumped by 30 percentage points of GDP during 1990–93, with the surge exacerbated by the substantial costs of recapitalizing the banking sector.

The resulting output losses proved to be permanent. Cerra and Saxena (2000) decompose output, unemployment, and inflation into common permanent, common temporary, and idiosyncratic components. Introducing two state variables to allow regime switching in the common permanent and common temporary components, it is shown that there was a permanent output loss associated with the recession in the early 1990s (Figure 12).

Emergence of the High-Technology Sector

In recent years, a vibrant high-technology sector has emerged in Sweden. Regardless of any growth lag since 1960, Sweden ranks favorably among all countries of the world, along with other Nordic countries, in the development and use of information and communication technology (ICT). This raises the possibility that there are significant "new economy" developments in Sweden, which was ranked by the International Data Corporation as the leading ICT nation in both 1999 and 2000. Sweden's advanced position is due to a large extent to the success of Ericsson, the largest ICT company in Sweden, the world's largest producer of mobile networks, and the third largest supplier of handsets. In addition to its high position in the development and production of information and communications technologies, Sweden also ranks high in the usage of these technologies. The ministry of finance calculated in its spring 2001 budget that the ICT sector contributed roughly a third of the growth in GDP and in exports and at least a quarter of that in productivity over the period 1994–2000 (Figures 13 and 14).

Several factors contributed to Sweden's high position in the ICT sector. Ericsson and the public telecommunications monopoly, Telia, invested early in establishing a mobile network (Figure 15). They designed the first generation of a mobile network in the 1970s, the Nordic Mobile Telephony, which was launched in 1981 as a Scandinavia-wide mobile system. Ericsson and Telia also introduced the digital Global System for Mobile Communications (GSM) in 1992, which became the most widely used mobile phone standard. High expenditure on research and development supported the development of the industry. Sweden was also one of the first countries in Europe to deregulate the telecommunications market, which spurred competition and helped establish a GSM mobile phone system throughout the country. In addition, there were a number of public incentives for the adoption of ICT, such as government subsidies to allow employees to lease computers from their employers for home use. Sweden's openness facilitated trade, and high public expenditure on education contributed to a highly skilled labor force, benefiting the ICT industries. Finally, labor relations in Sweden have generally been productive and free of strife (Figures 16 and 17).

While the bursting of the ICT bubble has imposed substantial costs on the sector in Sweden since late 2000, its long-term position remains promising. The period of explosive demand growth projections and associated booming capital spending in the ICT sector was reversed from early 2001. This has severely affected Ericsson and, given its large weight in market capitalization on the Stockholm stock exchange (about one-third in 2000), the Swedish equity market as well. Large sales of Ericsson stock by foreigners may have also contributed to the substantial weakening of the krona during the same period. However, Ericsson has been chosen as sole or cosupplier of networks for one or more of the 3G licensees in the all-important West Eu-

Figure 13. Top Ten Information Technology (IT) Countries, 2001
(IDC/World Times scores)

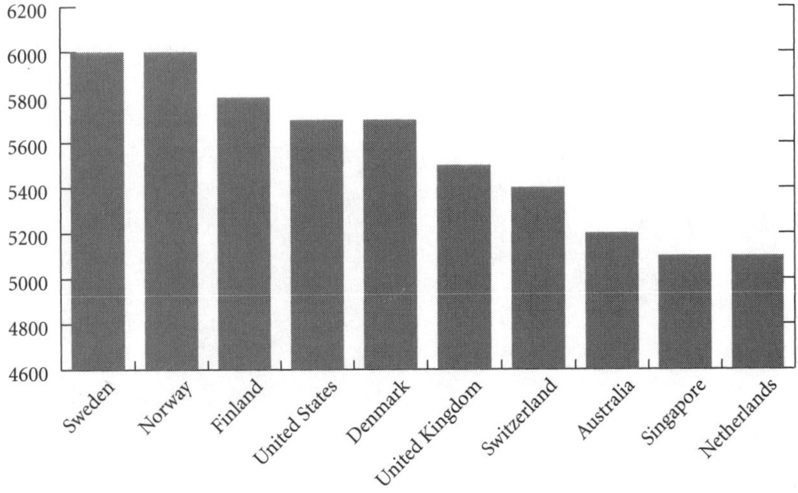

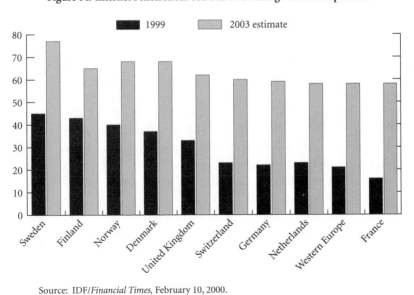

Source: IDC/*World Times* Survey 2001.

Figure 14. Internet Penetration: Users as a Percentage of Total Population

Source: IDF/*Financial Times*, February 10, 2000.

Figure 15. Investments in IT and Telecommunications, 2000
(In percent of GDP)

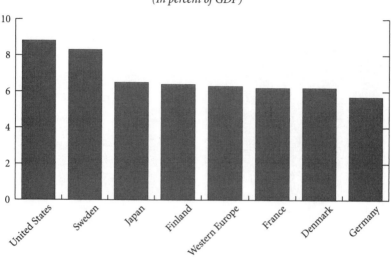

Source: EITO, 2001.

ropean markets (except Austria),[19] and also has strong positions in Asia and other important markets. This holds the promise that Sweden's ICT sector will regain its shine once the inevitable period of consolidation and rationalization of business practices in the sector is over.

High wage compression may have led to low labor costs for skilled workers, but in the long run it hampers the ability to attract and retain skilled workers. The ICT companies, and Ericsson in particular, are not outside the wage bargaining system and the level of unionization is not noticeably lower in the ICT sector than elsewhere in the economy. The resultant low wage dispersion may have enhanced the profitability of ICT companies, but over time it could erode their ability to recruit and retain highly skilled workers. Wage compression lowers the absolute and relative return to investment in human capital, necessitating significant subsidies for public education. Progressive taxation adds to the problem. If an engineer was paid a U.S.-style salary in Sweden, the total labor costs including social security contributions, the bulk of which are closer to taxes in nature, would be excessively high. This system is open to exploitation by obtaining subsidized higher education, then leaving Sweden to reap much higher after-tax salaries abroad. At the highest ranks, ICT companies

---

[19]*Financial Times*, "Telecoms Survey," January 23, 2002.

Figure 16. Public Expenditure on Education
(In percent of GDP)

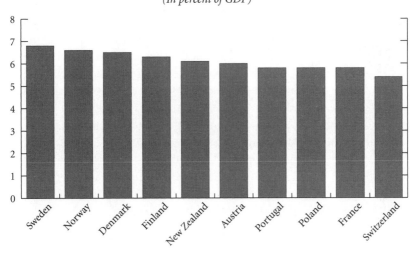

Source: OECD (2000).

**Figure 17. Literacy Skills: Percentage of Population (Aged 16 to 65)
at the Highest Literacy Level**

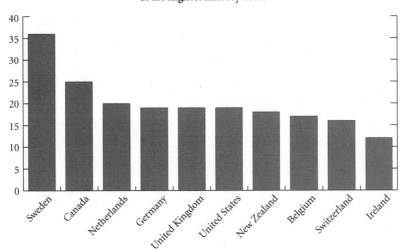

Source: OECD, *Education at Glance* (Paris, 2000).

have used other means to stimulate performance, notably stock options, which were also a feature of remunerating top people in the financial sector. According to the Union of Industrial and Employer's Confederations of Europe (UNICE) benchmarking report, however, Swedish employees would pay in tax 53 percent of the gains from a typical stock option program, compared with only 20 percent in the United States, and less than 10 percent in Belgium.

Much of the windfall from positive developments of Swedish enterprises (such as a surge in productivity) increasingly accrues to foreigners. The proportion of foreign-owned shares on the Stockholm stock exchange more than quadrupled in the 1990s to over 38 percent in 2000. To the extent that this trend is caused by a desire for greater diversification, it can help shield Sweden from volatile wealth effects of a technology-based equity market. Yet the pattern of ownership of Swedish stocks is probably also heavily influenced by tax considerations. The reasonable level of corporate income tax combined with a very high taxation of savings by Swedish investors—discussed in Chapter 6—implies that foreigners will tend to own a large share of Swedish stocks, and hence to obtain an increasing proportion of the associated gains (or losses) (Figures 18 and 19).

Overall, the outlook for Sweden's ICT sector remains promising, especially if labor market incentives, particularly for skilled workers, are improved. While underlying demand growth for ICT services and equipment for the coming years, and indeed for the longer term, has been scaled down from earlier overly optimistic levels, the sector remains a huge and relatively high-growth segment of the world economy. Policies conducive to increasing incentives to attract and retain highly skilled workers and stemming outflows of domestic capital seeking tax havens may be needed, however, to help Swedish suppliers retain and solidify their early lead in ICT, especially in mobile communications. Such policies would include measures to facilitate greater labor market flexibility and greater wage dispersion, as well as rationalizing taxes on savings and wealth (as discussed in Chapter 6).

Quality of Growth

Higher output and faster growth do not necessarily imply higher levels of economic well-being. Even if Sweden's growth has lagged, its quality of life is consistently ranked high: fourth in the world, for example (after Norway, Australia, and Canada), according to the UN's 2000 *Human Development Report* survey (UNDP, 2000).

Sweden has also attached importance to, and done much to achieve, high environmental quality. In terms of the environmental sustainability index—

Figure 18. Foreign Ownership of Stockholm Stock Exchange, 1991–2000

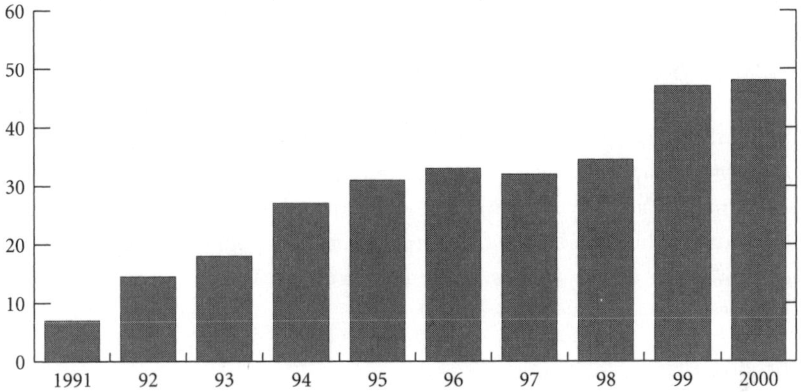

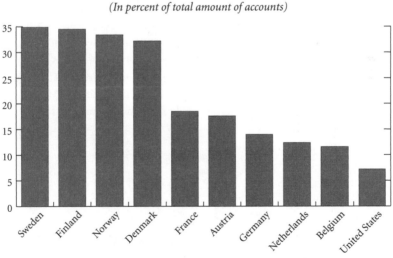

Source: SIS Agarseervice, AB.

Figure 19. Online Banking: Internet Accounts
(In percent of total amount of accounts)

Source: IDC (2001).

the most comprehensive measure of progress toward environmental sustainability—Sweden ranks among the top 4 of 122 countries; in its commitment to research and development and protection of the global environment, Sweden is ranked at the top. At 17 percent of GDP, genuine savings—savings

taking account of environmental degradation, the depletion of the natural resource base, and the acquisition of human capital—are 3 percentage points
above the OECD average. Sweden continues to refine its environmental policy
framework. A 1997 government bill outlined 15 environmental policy goals for
the next 25 years, with an aim of promoting an ecologically sustainable development through legislation and balanced fiscal incentives. In pursuit of these
goals, a new environmental code entered into force in 1999, representing a body
of coordinated and more stringent environmental legislation. Moreover, the
2001 and 2002 budgets included revenue-neutral tax policy changes to further
reduce Sweden's already low greenhouse gas emissions.

Conclusions

The basic facts seem relatively straightforward. Sweden's relative position has
declined since the mid-1960s, due to a combination of a convergence process
as others caught up with Sweden's earlier gains, and policy mistakes that led to
permanent output losses. More recently, growth has been spurred by a flour-
ishing high-tech sector. Above all, perhaps, Sweden has come to score highly
on almost all indicators of economic performance that are more broadly defined than on simple income measures.

It is hard to avoid the impression that much of the controversy on Sweden's
relative growth performance reflects differing underlying positions as to the
effects of the Swedish welfare state. If that is the real controversy, it is better addressed directly rather than by seeking inferences from simple analysis of
trends. The next chapter attempts to provide such an assessment of Sweden's
growth performance.

4 Growth, Government, and the Welfare State

Whatever one's view of Sweden's relative growth performance over past decades, it could be, nevertheless, that Sweden's growth performance is substantially dependent on the extent and quality of government intervention. This chapter draws on the large body of theoretical and empirical work on the determinants of growth to address this question.[20] Some methodological points need to be stressed at the outset.

- It is important to distinguish between different aspects of growth. The welfare state may have affected the level of output in Sweden, but not the long-run rate of growth. In the neoclassical growth model, for instance, the long-run growth rate is determined by (supposedly) exogenous factors, such as the rates of population growth and technological progress, so that government could affect the rate of growth only in the short run, with potentially permanent effects on the output level. In more recent endogenous growth models, on the other hand, public policies that impact productivity or incentives to invest in human and physical capital can permanently alter the long-run rate of growth. The consequences of these two kinds of effects—on levels and growth—are quite different. As Atkinson (1999) stresses, however, it can be difficult to distinguish empirically between them: it can take a long time to know whether a change or difference in growth rates is permanent or transitory.

- More growth is not necessarily better: a country may grow faster than is optimal in terms of its citizens' welfare, not only because of the adverse

---

[20]Recent surveys include Aghion, Caroli, and Garcia-Peñalosa (1999); Gerson (1998); Masson (2000); and Tanzi and Zee (1997).

environmental effects that may be associated with growth (commented on in the final section of the previous chapter) but also because savings and work effort may cost more in the loss of present consumption and leisure than they are worth in terms of increased output; and consumers may be willing to accept some reduction in their income levels if that is the price to pay for achieving their equity objectives.[21]

We return to several of these caveats below.

Growth and the Basic Functions of Government

There seem to have been few direct studies of the impact of government on growth in Sweden. This is not surprising, since there is relatively little time-series variation to exploit in the recent past. There is, however, a large empirical literature drawing primarily on cross-country variation. Thus our approach in what follows is to ask how Sweden measures up against factors identified in that wider literature as significant for growth.

Two factors that repeatedly appear as important determinants of growth are education and health. Several studies find a positive relationship between high levels of education achievement and growth,[22] or—more directly relevant to the role of government—between public spending on education and growth.[23] Using a Bayesian averaging technique, Doppelhofer, Miller, and Sala-i-Martin (2000) find evidence that primary education and life expectancy are among the robust determinants of growth in a random sample of approximately 21 million of the possible regressions that include any combination of 32 conditioning variables. However, they did not test whether *spending* on schooling and health is robustly related to productivity enhancement, and other empirical studies provide mixed conclusions. The relationship may be hard to verify because the levels of health and educational attainment may not be proxied well by expenditures on these items. In addition, it may take many years before spending can feed through to higher achievement levels and productivity growth.

Sweden rates highly in terms of both the quality of its workforce and health measures. It scored highest in the three main domains of literacy skills in the

---

[21]Nor indeed is growth even synonymous with "efficiency," a term used in this book in the sense of Pareto efficiency, referring to a situation in which it is impossible to make any one person better off without making any other worse off.

[22]Including Denison (1967) and Barro (1989).

[23]Diamond (1989); Otani and Villanueva (1990); Hansson and Henrekson (1994); Barro and Sala-i-Martin (1995); and Tanzi (1995).

OECD's International Adult Literacy Survey published in 2000; and three-quarters of all adults have graduated from high school, the highest rate in the OECD. Sweden also tops the list of 94 countries in the State of the World index covering 10 key factors of women's and children's health, education, and political status. Swedes' overall level of health, measured by disability-adjusted life expectancy, is the fourth highest in the world.[24] Sweden ties with Japan for the highest life expectancy among the poor; and, finally, the country ranks fourth in the world, after Norway, Australia, and Canada, and ahead of the United States (sixth), in quality of life, according to the 2000 survey by the UN Development Program.[25] (The survey, published annually since 1990, combines measures of per capita income, health care, life expectancy, and educational levels.)

How far government intervention is responsible for these achievements is open to debate. On the face of it, incentives to human capital formation might seem to be considerably blunted by both the tradition of quite steeply progressive income taxation and wage compression, both of which reduce the return to forgoing income when young in order to earn more when older. This is to some degree offset, however, by such other measures as those encouraging high rates of labor force participation, and hence the development and maintenance of work skills.

There is also substantial evidence that government spending on maintaining a stable political and legal framework and an effective bureaucracy can facilitate growth. The key channels through which it does this are the reduction in private investment risk and the encouragement of innovation. Concerns about expropriation or loss of property discourage investment and divert resources to less productive but more secure investments. A number of empirical studies[26] find that political unrest and instability and corruption have significant negative effects on growth. In theory, defense spending could have a positive impact on growth by reducing political instability or by providing "spin-off" effects of technological improvement, provision of infrastructure, or education of soldiers. However, military expenditure could also crowd out spending on health, education, and civilian infrastructure, as well as savings for private investment. Overall, the empirical literature shows a negative or insignificant relationship between defense spending and growth.[27]

---

[24]World Health Organization (2000).
[25]UNDP (2000), available at *http://www.undp.org/hdr2000/*.
[26]Barro (1991); Alesina and Rodrik (1992); and Easterly and Rebelo (1993).
[27]Landau (1993) finds evidence that the impact may be nonlinear, with low (high) defense spending enhancing (inhibiting) growth.

Political stability in Sweden has evidently been high, as—in general—has the quality and transparency with which the public sector has been managed. This in turn has reflected the social consensus at the heart of the welfare state itself. In the best of times, Sweden thus seems to have established a happy equilibrium, in which the welfare state itself may have cemented a stability conducive to growth. This stability was shaken, however, by the crisis of the early 1990s, when the underlying fiscal position veered towards unsustainability, leading—as noted above—to a permanent loss of output.

Public expenditure on capital items can in principle enhance output and/or growth to the extent that it is of a kind that, because of some external effects, would not be undertaken at a proper level by the private sector. However, the empirical evidence on the effects of government capital expenditure on growth is mixed. The results depend on the sample and specification, and studies have often not distinguished between types of capital expenditure. Easterly and Rebelo (1993) do differentiate between types of capital expenditure in a large sample covering 119 countries from the 1960s through the 1980s, and find that public investment in transport and communications improves growth without crowding out private investment; investment in public enterprises has no effect; and public investment in agriculture has a negative effect. Estimated elasticities of growth with respect to public infrastructure investment have tended to be small. This suggests some caution in supposing Sweden to have enjoyed substantial growth effects from high infrastructure expenditure. However, Martin (2000) cites evidence that regional infrastructure investment in telecommunications—which has been an especially well-served sector in Sweden, as discussed below—has a more favorable effect on growth in Europe than other types of infrastructure investment. Berndt and Hansson (1992) find that infrastructure investment had a significant impact on Swedish productivity, however, allowing a lower labor requirement for firms. As for research and development investment, the evidence is also mixed. It appears to be important for productivity growth at the firm level (Griliches, 1991), but the effect at the national level appears to differ with the stage of development: Coe and Helpman (1993) find that domestic investment in research and development contributes significantly to TFP growth in Group of Seven (G-7) countries, but research and development investment has generally not been significant for middle-income and developing countries (which may benefit more from domestic competition and the importation of new technologies). Even in industrial countries, however, publicly sponsored research and development does not appear to significantly affect output growth.

Growth and the Welfare State

Perhaps the most crucial issue in assessing the impact of government on growth in Sweden, however, is the effect of the extensive tax transfer interventions in support of large-scale redistribution. This depends on the balance between negative and positive effects.

The potential for negative effects on output and growth is well known. Labor income taxes tilt the balance, at the margin, towards taking leisure rather than working, and progressive taxation discourages human capital accumulation by taxing the returns to increased future wages at a higher rate than the implicit expenditure on acquiring that capital (reduced wages when young) can be deducted against tax. Corporate taxes may discourage capital accumulation, and taxes on capital income at the personal level may distort savings decisions. A proportional tax on consumption—such as a uniform VAT—will have quite similar effects to a tax on wage income but does not distort the savings decision or incentives to invest in human or physical capital (since it leaves the relative price of current versus future consumption and wages unchanged). Nevertheless, by increasing the cost of market-produced goods, it may reduce lifetime labor supply and increase home production, impacting on growth through the attendant decrease in the average productivity of the working-age population. In addition, some types of social transfers, such as generous programs of unemployment, sickness, or early retirement, can discourage job search, reduce labor supply, and keep the recipients mired in a poverty trap. Many of these effects are addressed in detail in later chapters. But there are also a number of ways in which redistribution can improve growth, and we return to some of these shortly.

At a fairly aggregate level, the links between taxes, spending, redistribution, and growth have received considerable attention in recent years. A number of studies have found a positive relationship between public transfers or income equality and growth.[28] Benabou (1996) compared the Philippines and Korea, which had similar macroeconomic indicators in the early 1960s. In the subsequent 30 years, the more equal Korea grew fivefold, while the output level of the Philippines barely doubled. Alesina and Perotti (1996) find evidence that inequality creates social unrest and political instability, which, as noted above, depress investment and growth. However, the direction of causality between redistribution and growth is difficult to ascertain. Faster-growing countries may be able to afford more generous social assistance schemes. The relation-

---

[28]Including Alesina and Rodrik (1994); Barro (1989); Persson and Tabellini (1994); and Sala-i-Martin (1992).

ship may also depend on the level of development, with inequality in poor countries contributing to poor health and lack of schooling. The empirical evidence is mixed for OECD countries. Some studies[29] find a significant negative effect of various measures of social transfers on growth in samples of OECD countries, whereas other studies find a positive effect.[30]

The empirical evidence on the effects of tax rates on per capita income growth is thus inconclusive. There are several econometric problems that could be responsible for the vastly different results. The size of the public sector tends to increase with the level of development, and wealthier countries tend to rely more on income and payroll taxes and less on trade taxes than do developing countries (Easterly and Rebelo, 1993). Therefore, studies of the effect of the structure and size of government on growth are likely to be affected by reverse causality. This occurs because the initial level of per capita GDP is negatively correlated with growth due to output convergence. Output convergence occurs in exogenous growth models due to diminishing returns to capital, but it can also occur in endogenous growth models due to knowledge or technological spillovers or product imitation across countries. The results of studies that do not control for initial income are particularly likely to be biased. Another problem is that many studies that include the tax ratio in a growth regression do not distinguish between different types of more or less distorting taxes nor for the more or less productive expenditure uses of the revenue. Finally, even if taxes have a significant impact on growth, they could still have a negative effect on welfare due to their deadweight losses.

Partial studies investigating the effects of fiscal policy on growth that focus on one side of the government's budget constraint can be severely biased and lead to a perception that the evidence is nonrobust. Kneller, Bleaney, and Gemmell (1999) stress that much of the earlier empirical work needs to be reassessed because of an incomplete specification of the government budget constraint. For example, Mendoza, Milesi-Ferretti, and Asea (1997) conclude that the tax mix has no significant effect on growth, but since their regressions do not include expenditure variables, their estimates are biased by the implicit partial financing of productive expenditures. Likewise, several studies on expenditure fail to include tax variables to control for the distortionary financing of the expenditure. Kneller, Bleaney, and Gemmell examine a panel of 22 OECD countries over 1970–95, looking for growth effects from the levels and

---

[29]Hansson and Henrekson (1994); Nordström (1992); Persson and Tabellini (1994); and Weede (1986, 1991).

[30]Castles and Dowrick (1990), Korpi (1985), and McCallum and Blais (1987) find a non-monotonic relationship.

structures of both taxation and expenditure. They aggregate a functional classification of fiscal data into four categories, which they label—in somewhat judgmental terms—as "distortionary" taxation (taxes on income and profit, social security contributions, taxes on payroll and manpower, and taxes on property); "nondistortionary" taxation (taxes on domestic goods and services); "productive" expenditures (general public services, defense, education, health, housing, transport, and communication); and "unproductive" expenditure (social security and welfare, recreation, and economic services). They find that the "distortionary" tax aggregate has a significant negative effect on growth, with an increase in revenue from these taxes of 1 percentage point of GDP causing growth to decline by 0.41 percentage points. A 1 percentage point increase in productive expenditure raises growth by 0.27 percentage points.[31] Nondistortionary taxes and unproductive expenditure, on the other hand, have no significant effect on growth.

Taken literally, this would imply, for instance, that if Sweden had reduced taxes other than the VAT by 2 percentage points of GDP and preserved budget balance by cutting transfers, annual growth would have increased by about 0.8 percentage points; implying, if sustained over 20 years, an increase in real income of over 17 percent. Or, by switching 2 percentage points of expenditure from transfers to health and education, growth could have been increased by about 0.5 percentage points. But such empirical exercises are not to be taken so literally. Apart from a range of technical issues, by their nature they ignore a host of detail likely to be important in the circumstances of particular countries. The purpose of the following chapters is to analyze in some detail Swedish experience in relation to some of these key issues, concerning labor market interventions, investment, and savings. The rest of this chapter explores a distinct set of issues alluded to above: the possibility that redistribution in Sweden may have had, in at least some respects, beneficial effects on growth and/or efficiency.

There are a number of channels through which such effects might operate.[32] When individuals have altruistic preferences—for example, so that the better-off derive satisfaction from the well-being of the poor—the income of the poor acquires the characteristic of a public good, so that compulsory redistribution

---

[31]The relationship between the level of public expenditure and growth may well be nonmonotonic. Tanzi and Schuknecht (1995), for instance, argue that increased public expenditure may enhance growth up to some point, after which it becomes increasingly wasteful. Crafts (2000) suggests that the advanced European countries have moved to the point at which the favorable effects of government spending on growth are offset by the disincentive effects of taxation.

[32]See, for instance, the survey in Boadway and Keen (2000).

towards them can raise the welfare of all individuals. Such altruism is clearly one possible explanation for the extent of redistribution in Sweden, and also consistent with Sweden's high level of assistance for developing countries.

Redistribution can also increase efficiency to the extent that it is a response to the nonexistence, as a consequence of informational imperfections, of certain key markets. In particular, when capital markets are imperfect, redistribution may overcome liquidity constraints that hinder the socially profitable investment in human or other forms of capital by the least well-off (Banerjee and Newman, 1993); and, by reducing investors' need to rely on external finance, it can ease the holdup problem that leaves potential partners reluctant to support projects that may leave them in an ex post weaker bargaining position (Hoff and Lyon, 1995). How important these effects are likely to be in Sweden is unclear, however: capital markets are well developed, and relatively few individuals appear liquidity constrained.

A central but open question is the extent to which extensive social insurance in Sweden induces a beneficial increase in risk taking. In the absence of well-functioning insurance markets, risk-averse individuals are likely to underinvest in risky activities, choosing safer occupations or investments than they ideally would. Social insurance may then improve efficiency by encouraging risk taking (Sinn, 1995). Even a proportional income tax, for instance, reduces the riskiness of an undertaking by taxing away part of the high returns if it turns out well and implicitly bearing some of the cost if it turns out badly. A range of policy measures in Sweden may bear on risk taking, such as the availability of social assistance and unemployment benefit, and the knowledge that the benefit will be available to support one's children in all outcomes. While the potentially beneficial impact of social insurance on risk taking has attracted much theoretical attention, its practical importance is hard to gauge. There are some very tentative signs of relatively high risk taking in Sweden. Equity holdings are more extensive than in other countries.[33] One might also look for signs of risk taking in the start-up of new businesses. Comparing six developed countries, OECD (1994) reports Sweden as having the highest number of firm births per existing firm and the third highest number per person; and OECD (2002) reports venture capital, relative to GDP, as higher in Sweden than in any OECD country other than Iceland, the United Kingdom, and the United States. However, there are clearly many other factors potentially affecting these aspects of performance. Moreover, in a rare empirical examination of this important

---

[33]According to the March 30, 2001 issue of *Global Data Watch* (published by the Morgan Guaranty Trust), two-thirds of Swedes—double the European average—hold shares.

issue, Ilmakunnas and Kannainen (2001) find that in OECD countries social insurance tends, if anything, to reduce entrepreneurship and risk taking. The important question of how the welfare state affects risk taking, in Sweden and elsewhere, deserves closer attention.

Conclusions

The links between growth and government intervention are evidently complex, and still imperfectly understood—both in general and with respect to Sweden. Perhaps the clearest conclusion to emerge is the need to guard against simplistic conclusions. It is worth bearing in mind, for instance, that although Sweden's ranking and relative per capita output have declined, there were other countries with a similarly significant decline in their relative positions (such as Australia, United Kingdom, and New Zealand) that did not follow the Nordic model of public policy.

Nevertheless, there is good reason to suppose that the high levels of taxation in Sweden—especially, for reasons that will emerge in later chapters, on labor income—have depressed growth. And it is certainly possible to argue that Sweden's large welfare state may have created institutional rigidities that interacted with policy and exogenous shocks, amplifying their effects and making them more permanent, thus preventing the economy from fully rebounding from the severe recession of the early 1990s.[34] There is no very firm empirical evidence, on the other hand, that the high level of transfers has in itself significantly depressed growth. Indeed, several aspects of the Swedish welfare state seem to be conducive to growth; certainly the emergence of the strong high-tech sector shows Swedish institutional structures to be consistent with remarkably strong growth performance. At the most fundamental level, the powerful role given to government in Sweden reflects a strong social consensus whose economic expression tends to provide a stability that is itself supportive of continued growth.

---

[34]Blanchard and Wolfers (1999) argue that this has been true of European labor markets more generally. In addition to labor market rigidities, relevant institutional aspects of the Swedish model include product market rigidities, disincentives stemming from high taxes and transfers, and extensive regulatory intervention.

5 Labor Market Interventions

Policymakers in Sweden have long seen the shaping of labor market outcomes as critical to the pursuit of their equity objectives, using a range of instruments—both fiscal and nonfiscal—to secure high and stable levels of employment together with extensive participation. This chapter reviews experience with the principal devices used to these ends.

Background: A Brief History of Labor Market Outcomes

Centralized bargaining, a pivotal component of the Swedish model, aimed for full employment at high participation rates both as a means to income security within an egalitarian distribution of labor income and in order to broaden the tax base and hence help finance high budgetary expenditures. While these goals had largely been achieved through the mid-1980s, as welfare arrangements grew in size so the long-term disincentive effects of the Swedish model became more apparent. These effects stemmed from growing tax wedges, increasingly generous transfers, legislation raising the cost of firing and hiring, a high effective floor on the wage level, and growing uncertainty about the real value of future welfare entitlements as public debt grew rapidly. The result was a period of latent increases in unemployment (with the consensus estimate of the equilibrium unemployment rate steadily rising throughout the 1980–93 period) followed by a sudden quadrupling of the open unemployment rate during 1990–93 to 8 percent. The macroeconomic crisis hit employment and brought the public employment boom—which boosted public employment from 15 percent of the labor force in 1970 to one-third in the early 1990s—to an end. Awareness of these structural weaknesses was a key factor in the consensus underlying the 1991 tax reform summarized in Box 2 (in Chapter 2), with the restructuring of the labor income tax estimated by both Agell, Englund, and Södersten (1998) and Blomquist, Elköf, and Newey (2001) to have led to an increase in labor supply on the order of 2 percent. Following the deep recession of the early 1990s, steady improvements have been registered in employment, unemployment, and participation rates. The levels of the late 1980s, however, have not been recovered. Participation rates, for example, remained 7 percent lower in 2000 than a decade earlier, with a drop of over one-fifth for workers under age 25.

Assessing the Impact of Government

A wide range of policy measures impact a variety of labor market outcomes. The state affects the labor market through the tax transfer system, through its influence on wage bargaining institutions and outcomes, and through spending on labor market programs. These potentially bear on all key dimensions of labor market performance, including hours worked, participation decisions, the duration of unemployment spells, the intensity of search effort, absenteeism, and the acquisition of human capital. These are areas, moreover, in which there has been substantial policy change over the past decade or so. Not surprisingly, the labor market impact of intervention in Sweden has been widely discussed and studied over this period. This section offers an overview of some of the principal issues and conclusions.

Incentives and the Tax Transfer System

The most direct (and readily quantified) effects are those of the tax transfer system on labor market incentives. Assessing these incentives, which bear on labor market outcomes, requires taking account of a wide range of features of the tax transfer system:

- Local income tax payable beyond a low basic allowance, at rates between 26 and 34 percent and averaging a little over 30 percent. Central income tax becomes payable at 20 percent on taxable income of SKr 273,800, and at 25 percent above SKr 414,200.[35] These latter thresholds are high, so that only about 9 percent of full-time employees pay central income tax.

- Social security contributions payable at 32.82 percent by employers, and at 7 percent (up to SKr 301,011) by employees themselves. To the extent that these are not perceived to carry actuarially fair benefits, the incentive effects of these will be akin to a tax. The ministry of finance estimates that over half of the average contribution could be regarded as a tax in this sense.

---

[35]There is no deduction or credit of either tax against the other.

- Indirect taxes—not least a standard VAT rate of 25 percent—affecting individuals' budget constraints in much the same way as taxes on their labor income, and so having, in principle, similar incentive effects.

- The withdrawal of means-tested benefits as income rises reduces disposable income just as would an explicit tax. As stressed in Chapter 2, Sweden has no general in-work benefit explicitly structured as a supplement to low incomes. Social assistance payments are available, however, to guarantee a minimum level of income to all, with an implicit tax (at a marginal rate of 100 percent) as income rises towards that level. Social assistance is paid by local governments, which have some discretion over its level. Moreover, housing allowances and the subsidy to childcare payments are means tested. So too is the repayment of student loans, again having an effect—once the benefits of the loan have already been enjoyed—similar to an explicit tax.

- Contingent benefit payments for unemployment, sickness, and parental duties, which potentially affect decisions on labor market status. These are typically related to prior earnings, and so may also affect the work effort of those likely to fall into these contingencies.

These taxes and transfers potentially distort labor market decisions by driving a wedge between the cost to the employer of expanding employment and the real value of the resources that the associated net earnings will buy the worker. When the former exceeds the latter, society loses from dissipation of the otherwise mutually beneficial expansion of employment that the tax transfer system frustrates. Such distortions operate on a variety of margins.

Hours Worked

Much attention traditionally focuses, in Sweden as elsewhere, on the impact of policy on workers' decisions as to the number of hours worked. In the short term, of course, many workers have relatively little control over the hours they work, especially given the existence of institutional limits on the number of hours of overtime that can be worked (some specified in national laws, others in central or firm-level agreements). Over the medium term, however, there is scope for variation in the renegotiation of labor agreements.

The impact of the tax transfer system on hours worked depends on both the average and the marginal rates of taxes and transfers combined, with the former critical for participation decisions and the latter for the level of effort chosen by those in work. Conditional on having chosen to participate in the labor market, the average tax rate—likely to be negative at low incomes, with benefits received exceeding taxes paid—determines the "income effect" of the system. The higher the proportion of income taken in tax, the less the household can afford to take leisure, and so the greater on this account will be its labor supply. The average rate will also affect the discrete choices as to whether to work at all and of whether to migrate. The marginal tax rate, on the other hand, determines the "substitution effect": the higher it is, the less is the return from additional earnings, and so the lower labor supply will be. While the overall outcome depends on both marginal and average rates, the two differ crucially in their welfare significance. Since the income effect arises from the need to raise revenue, it is in a sense inescapable: even the least distorting tax system would generate an income effect. Thus, conditional on participation, it is only the marginal rate that generates efficiency losses; and it is with this that we begin.

The extent of the distortion to labor market incentives at the margin is conveniently described by the marginal effective labor income tax rate (MELT), defined as the proportion of one additional krona of earnings that is offset by increased tax payments and the withdrawal of benefit. Simple calculations show that this can be substantial in Sweden. For a worker paying at the top central marginal tax rate, the combined effect of income tax, the average VAT, and employer's social security contributions is a MELT on the order of 71 percent.[36] That is, SKr 100 additional expense by the employer buys the worker goods worth only SKr 29. For those lower down the income scale, the impact of the income tax will be less, but the withdrawal of means-tested benefits (particularly housing allowance and childcare support) will tend to raise the MELT.

MELTs on labor income in Sweden are high over some income ranges and for some household types. This is illustrated in Figure 20, which shows the MELT associated with social security contributions, central and local income taxes, housing allowances, and childcare support for single-earner households differing in the number of children. (Note that housing allowances and, of course, childcare support are not available to those without children.) The figure shows that the impact of these contributions and taxes is much less straightforward than might have been supposed. In particular, the MELT from these sources at some points actually falls with income, running counter to the

---

[36]Assuming all income to arise from wages, and that there is no savings, the consumer's budget constraint implies that $(1 + v)C = (1 - \tau_w)W$, where C denotes consumption, W wage income, v the uniform rate of consumption tax (taken to be 17.6 percent), and τ_w the rate of income taxation (55 percent). The gross cost to the employer of hiring this worker, G, is $(1 + \tau_s)W$, where τ_s is the rate of the employer's social security contribution (32.92 percent). Combining the two, the MELT, defined as unity minus the derivative of consumption with respect to the employer's wage cost, is $1 - (1 - 0.55)/[(1 + 0.3292)(1 + 0.176)]$. When, as in practice, taxes are nonlinear, the same algebra applies at the margin.

Figure 20. MELTs for a Single Earner in 2001

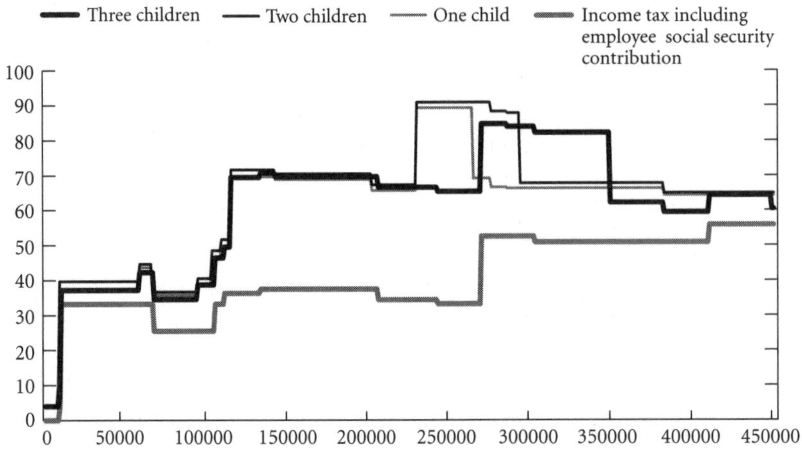

Source: Ministry of Finance.

usual notion that the marginal tax rate ought to increase with income.[37] The most striking downward dip reflects an unusual feature of the Swedish tax system—resulting from changes made in the 1991 tax reform—that, over a range of low incomes, the allowance (i.e., the standard deduction from taxable income) actually increases with income.[38] However, income tax and social security are not the only important determinants of the MELT. The withdrawal of means-tested housing and childcare benefits can give rise to very high MELTs at lower levels of income: well over 60 percent over quite a wide range, and in some cases even over 90 percent. Although the absence of means-tested income supplements means that these MELTs are, in a broad sense, lower than is sometimes found, they clearly have the potential to create significant disincentives to work among some groups of low-wage earners.

---

[37]There is in theory no reason to require the MELT to rise everywhere with income. Indeed, optimal tax schedules in some key cases imply that it should fall over high income ranges (Seade, 1977). More generally, although theory warns that optimal marginal effective rate schedules can have all kinds of shapes—see for instance the various cases in Boadway, Cuff, and Marchand (2000) for which closed-form solutions are obtained—there is no generally compelling rationale for having the MELT fall over a range of low incomes and then rise again.

[38]It then declines back to its initial level, implying a MELT initially below and then above the statutory tax rate. The purpose of this measure was to reduce marginal tax rates for those with very low incomes, especially students and part-time working mothers. However, this came at the cost of imposing particularly high marginal tax rates on those with somewhat higher incomes.

Table 7. Average Marginal Effective Labor Income Tax Rate (MELT)
Across Households, 2001
(In percent)

Total	45.5
Of which	
Income tax	34.5
Childcare	0.2
Housing allowance	1.5
Social assistance	1.6
Maintenance advance	0.2
Unemployment insurance	7.6

Source: Ministry of Finance.

Averaged across all households—and in this calculation ignoring both the employers' social security contributions and indirect taxes—the marginal effective tax rate is about 46 percent. Table 7 shows the average MELT for a hypothetical increase of SKr 12,000 in the earnings of all households (and thus includes the effects of moving from unemployment back to work, an issue addressed below), together with a decomposition into its underlying components. Such an average clearly conceals important interhousehold variation in the MELT, and will tend to understate the effective distortion of the labor supply decisions.[39]

While the MELT provides a conceptually sharp quantification of the strength of disincentives to marginal labor effort, the key policy question is the extent of the welfare losses from these disincentives. It is these efficiency costs that need to be weighed against any distributional gains. The extent of these losses depends on both the size of the MELT and, for the reasons given above, the strength of substitution effects, as measured by the compensated wage elasticity[40] of the supply of labor. By way of illustration, Table 8 reports figures for the marginal excess burden of labor income taxes at various levels of the MELT and at various plausible levels of the compensated wage elasticity for primary earners in Sweden. Elasticities for secondary earners are generally found to be higher. As can be seen from Figure 20, the range of assumed values for the MELT is also within the experience of many workers in Sweden.

[39]Since the excess burden of a tax is a convex function of the tax rate, the associated inefficiency when MELTs vary around an average will be greater than it would be if all households faced that average MELT.

[40]This is the elasticity when the consumer's income from nonlabor sources is adjusted so as to leave their level of well-being unaffected by the change in the wage rate.

Table 8. Marginal Excess Burden of Taxation (MEB) per Additional
SKr 100 of Revenue
(In percent)

MELT	Compensated Wage Elasticity of Labor Supply (ε)		
	0.05	0.11	0.25
35	2.7	6.2	15.4
46	4.4	10.1	26.5
60	7.9	19.1	57.3
70	12.5	32.5	125.9
80	22.7	68.8	1,250.0
90	61.6	521.0	−210[1]

Source: Authors' calculations.

Note: Marginal excess burden is calculated as $[t/(1-t)]\varepsilon/\{1 - [t/(1-t)](\varepsilon + \alpha\eta)\}$, where t is the marginal effective tax rate, ε the compensated wage elasticity, and η the income elasticity of labor supply (taken to be −0.05—in line with estimates for Sweden reported by Agell, Englund, and Södersten (1998)—and to be independent of the net wage) and α is the ratio of hours worked to the time endowment (assumed to be 0.4). Excess burden is defined as in Kay (1980). Nonlabor income is assumed to be zero, and there are no taxes other than on earned income.

[1]In this case, an increase in the tax rate actually reduces revenue, so that revenue can be increased while reducing excess burden.

At high MELTs, the efficiency loss is considerable even when compensated labor supply is relatively unresponsive. At a marginal effective rate of 80 percent, for example, even with a compensated elasticity as low as 0.05, the additional excess burden created by raising an additional SKr 1 of revenue is over SKr 0.2. In this context it should be emphasized that the 1991 tax reform, although to some degree reversed since (by, for instance, the introduction of the 7 percent employee's social security contribution), has greatly reduced the distortionary cost. Agell, Englund, and Södersten (1998) report, for example, that the MELT on the average blue collar worker was reduced from about 73 percent to about 63 percent by the reform, nearly halving the marginal excess burden per krona of revenue even at low levels of responsiveness. Nevertheless, the persistence of high MELTs means that there would still be a potentially worthwhile gain from further reducing MELTs. Even at the average current MELT of 46 percent, the marginal loss per krona of tax revenue may plausibly be as high as SKr 0.1–0.2.

The question of how to significantly reduce MELTs without unduly jeopardizing revenue or wider social objectives raises distinct issues at the top and bottom of the income distribution. It is here that incentive concerns are commonly greatest: in the former case reflecting a presumption that high earning power reflects an especially strong productive capacity; in the latter case in order to ensure that incentives for the poorest to improve their position by their own efforts are not blunted. Indeed, theory suggests—subject to many caveats—that the MELT should be zero at both extremes of the earnings distribution.[41]

Action at the top of the distribution is relatively easy. Simply eliminating the top central marginal rate of tax—establishing a uniform rate of 20 percent—would cost only about SKr 3 billion, roughly 0.3 percent of general government revenues. Going further and reducing the uniform central rate to 17 percent would only cost an additional SKr 5 billion.

It is more difficult to reduce the high MELTs at the lower end of the distribution, associated with the withdrawal of means-tested benefits and the relatively high starting rate of income tax. Simply adopting a slower phaseout for means-tested benefits in itself raises the cost of the benefit (the limiting case being that in which the benefits are paid to all, irrespective of income). Extending the range over which the benefit applies also raises MELTs above the income level at which the benefit would previously have been extinguished, making the problem of MELTs less marked but more widespread (although, since excess burden rises more than proportionately with the tax, this is likely to reduce the aggregate efficiency cost).[42] Offsetting these effects requires reducing the basic level of the benefit, and so reducing its distributional effectiveness at the lowest levels of income. Attention thus focuses naturally on the purpose of the means-tested benefits, and whether they might be better served by other instruments. The aim of providing acceptable housing for all, for example, might be better served by freeing up the housing market to allow for the expansion of affordable housing.

Since a key purpose of many of these means-tested benefits is to support households with children, a more efficient way of achieving the same end might be by increasing the flat-rate child benefit. This too would be costly in so far as these are paid to all with children, but some of the cost could be recouped by making the benefit taxable. For most households taxability would make little difference, since it would be possible to pay the same net amount at the same cost to the budget simply by grossing up the payment. In the higher reaches of the income distribution, however, where the income tax schedule is progressive, the net amount received would be lower, implying a more effective targeting of the benefit.

There may also be scope for moderating the impact of the income tax on low earners. The basic deduction from the income tax is very low, and the starting tax rate of 30 percent is relatively high by international standards (see

---

[41]This is shown in Edwards, Keen, and Tuomala (1994).

[42]MELTs may also need to rise to finance any increase in the costs of the benefit.

Table 3 in Chapter 2). Changes in these dimensions are liable to be costly, since an increased allowance or reduced starting rate would benefit all taxpayers. Indeed, the gain from increasing the allowance would be greatest for the highest earners, since it reduces the amount of income taxable at their highest marginal rate, and they are able to take maximum advantage of a reduced starting rate. Both effects could be limited, however, by transforming the basic allowance into a credit, the same for all. The state of the public finances is healthy enough to suggest that a start in this direction could be made in the foreseeable future.

Participation and Search Incentives

Public policy has been instrumental in attaining and maintaining high participation rates in Sweden. Participation rates are especially high for women and in the 50–64 age bracket, with participation rates for the latter being 12 percentage points above the OECD average. While the quite high average effective tax rates in Sweden—documented in discussing labor mobility in Chapter 8—would tend to discourage participation, a range of other measures act in the opposite direction. The elaborate and effective social support system for working parents and elderly workers, as well as the wide availability of part-time work, especially in the public sector, have played a key role. High marginal tax rates on the first earner and the direct link between wages and many social benefits also strongly encourage the labor force participation of the second earner in each family.

The unemployment benefit regime was made significantly more conducive to participation in early 2001. Prior to this, benefit duration spells could effectively be extended indefinitely by participation in labor market programs. This is no longer the case. Under the new "Activity Guarantee" scheme, at the end of a 300-day spell claimants who have not worked enough within that period to qualify for another 300-day benefit spell[43]—an extension that is available only once—are required to enter a full-time activity.[44]

At its current level of 80 percent—which was increased from 75 percent on September 1, 1997—however, the statutory replacement ratio remains high. While the effect of this has been mitigated by the SKr 580 ceiling on payments—which has remained unchanged for several years, and now constrains payments to about 45 percent of claimants—the increase in the ceiling to SKr 680 from July 2001 marks a significant increase in generosity. Past

---

[43]At least 70 hours per month for six months.

[44]Such activities may be offered during the benefit spell, with sanctions in the form of reduced benefit payment if not accepted.

experience suggests that this and other reforms to the unemployment benefit regime can have substantial behavioral effects: Carling, Holmlund, and Vejsiu (2001) find that the reduction in the replacement rate from 80 to 75 percent on January 1, 1996 increased transitions out of unemployment by around 10 percent.

Figure 21 compares the replacement rates for relatively low-paid workers across the EU, as of 1997, showing Sweden to have among the highest. This is especially so for households with children, reflecting a relatively high level of the child benefit.[45] Replacement rates are generally lower for higher-paid workers, reflecting the operation of the benefit ceiling, but those in Sweden again rank among the highest.

Disincentives to work are especially high among the low-paid with children. Calculations of replacement rates for representative workers of the kind reported in Figure 21 mask the considerable cross-household variation that can arise from the diversity of households' situations and the corresponding complexity of benefit arrangements. Table 9 shows not the replacement rate, but—a related quantity—the MELT (per krona of additional income) faced by workers moving into employment. This is over 90 percent for a low-paid worker with two children in daycare, reflecting a sharp withdrawal rate for the housing allowance and a marked increase in childcare costs. The MELT tends to be lower at higher incomes, reflecting the cap on the absolute amount of unemployment benefit paid. This creates an important disincentive to work by elevating the economic value of domestic work, general maintenance, and repairs that a household can perform for itself, as well as of taking paid work in the informal sector.

Sickness Benefits

Absences through sickness have increased substantially in recent years. The increase amounted to an average of 20,000[46] in 2000 compared with 1999, or 0.5 percent of total employment. There has been a strong procyclical movement in sickness absence in Sweden since the late 1960s (Aronsson and Walker, 1997), suggestive of work-related stress, compositional effects in the labor force (with those last employed having a higher propensity to be sick), or intertemporal smoothing of labor supply. But there is also evidence that, in Sweden as elsewhere, sickness absence is responsive to the incentive effects of the

---

[45]Payments received both in and out of work, such as child benefit, increase the replacement ratio (since they appear in both the numerator and denominator).

[46]Absent for the entire week owing to sickness.

Figure 21. Net Replacement Rates of the Unemployed at Average Wage Level, 1997

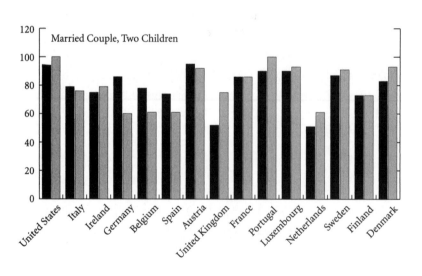

Source: OECD, *Benefit Systems and Work Incentives* (Paris, 1999).

benefit system (Johansson and Palme, 1993). Henrekson and Persson (2002) estimate that the 1998 increase in the sickness benefit replacement rate, from 75 to 80 percent, increased sick leave by about 30 percent.

Table 9. MELTs on Returning to Employment, 1999

Unemployment Benefit	Wage on Return to Employment	MELT	
		One child in daycare	Two children in daycare
96,000	120,000	64.1	92.7
150,800	192,000	63.4	70.1
150,800	300,000	54.8	57.6

Source: Ministry of Finance.

In this setting, the sickness benefit system is rightly coming under scrutiny. The restriction of unemployment benefit rules described above will increase the importance of guarding against an inappropriate expansion of sickness payments. In both the effectively unlimited duration of benefits and the level of compensation, however, the Swedish scheme is, by international standards, very generous (see, for instance, Mehrez, 2002). Not least, with employers bearing none of the cost after the first 14 days of a sickness spell, it may be difficult to guard against abuse. A natural strategy would be to improve employers' incentives to monitor absences more closely, either by increasing the periods for which they bear the cost of the benefit (from the present two weeks to, say, one month) or by introducing a system of experience rating (under which social security contributions would increase with the extent of their employees' claims).

Collective Bargaining and the Effects of the Tax Transfer System

The effective incidence of the tax transfer system can be much harder to gauge than is often supposed. Much discussion of the labor market impact of the tax transfer system—including that above—focuses on the effects on the incentives faced by individual workers, taking as given the wider labor market setting they face, their wage rates, the level of unemployment benefit, and so on. But that wider context is also liable to be affected by the tax transfer system, making it important to consider issues concerning its effective incidence. Part of the benefit of housing allowances, for instance, may accrue to landlords in the form of increased price of housing services; and employment subsidies may in part go to the benefit of employers, enabling them to pay reduced gross wages in the knowledge that they will be topped up by the state. Assessing effective incidence is difficult, and in many respects this remains an area of considerable ignorance.

Table 10. Average Direct Tax Rates by Income Group
(In percent)

	1989	1998
0–50,000	14	23
100,000–150,000	33	31
200,000–250,000	36	35
500,000–	58	43

Source: National Tax Board (2000).

One important determinant of that incidence, however, is the existence and nature of collective bargaining arrangements in the labor market. In particular:

- Under centralized wage bargaining, negotiators are more likely to be conscious of and hence internalize in their negotiating positions more of the macroeconomic risks—in terms of both unemployment and inflation—of high wage settlements.

- Progressivity of the tax transfer system is itself conducive to wage settlements that imply relatively low unemployment. The reason for this—an effect shown by Koskela and Vilmunen (1996) to apply in a range of bargaining models—is that a high marginal tax rate raises the before-tax cost to the employer of meeting any increase in after-tax wages, also raising the cost to the union, in terms of induced unemployment, of seeking such net wage increases. This tilts negotiations toward agreement involving relatively low wages and high employment. Empirical support for this effect has now been found in a range of countries, with Holmlund and Kolm (1995) finding such an effect for Sweden. As they note, this may be one reason why the positive correlation between labor taxes and unemployment found in an influential study by Daveri and Tabellini (2000) is not apparent in Sweden and the other Nordic countries.

Both of these effects, which mitigate the adverse employment consequences of the tax transfer system, have become less marked in recent years, with the bargaining system having become significantly less centralized since the 1970s (Friberg and Uddén-Sonnegård, 2001). The tax transfer system has also become less progressive since the 1991 reform: Table 10 shows a significant increase in the average direct taxes paid by the least well-off between 1989 and 1998, and a reduction in the average tax rate on the most well-off. Although it is hard to quantify the significance of these developments, their direction is fairly clear: the employment effects of the tax transfer system have become, through these routes, more adverse.

Wage Compression

Centralized bargaining in Sweden gave rise to a substantial compression of the wage scale, an implicit progressive tax on labor income akin to the explicit one. As shown in Figure 22,[47] wage compression in Sweden—as measured by the university wage premium—was at a level comparable to that in the United States in 1969, but it rose markedly in the 1980s, severely diminishing the private financial payoff to education. There has since been some decompression, but only enough to return to the level of 1969 and far below the current U.S. level.

By driving a wedge between relative wages and productivity differentials, wage compression generates distortions and consequent efficiency losses that are likely to be amplified by the progressivity of the tax transfer system. Indeed, Lindquist (2000) estimates that the potential welfare gain from removing wage compression would be around 4 percent of GDP, mainly due to higher employment of low-skill workers, and the resulting broader tax base and reduced need for transfers. The substitution effect of a wage scale compressed across skill levels reduces work intensity and hours worked by high-skill labor, and induces low-skill workers to work too much, impairing average productivity levels. Exacerbated by high and progressive labor taxation, it reduces the returns to education, and hence the incentives for acquiring education, lowering the average skill level. While the subsidization of education can counter this effect, it leads to inefficient resource utilization unless the positive externalities associated with higher education levels are commensurate. Wage compression also diminishes incentives for creating jobs for low-skilled workers, or for retaining them. A significantly compressed wage structure is invariably associated with a relatively high effective minimum wage (even when, as in Sweden, there is no legislated minimum wage), which hampers the entry of low-productivity workers, especially the young. Finally, the response of migration patterns to wage compression may result in a net loss of human capital.

A related problem is that relative wage adjustment is very sluggish in the present low-inflation environment, exacerbating the effect of the compressed wage structure. Nominal wages remain sticky in Sweden, with downward adjustments extremely rare even in a crisis.[48] The only exceptions are sector or individual specific. Nominal salary cuts have occurred in the ICT sector recently as a result of the worsening of the outlook in the sector. In addition, individuals may choose to trade off a higher but volatile income stream for a

---

[47]See also Table 19 in Chapter 8.
[48]Agell and Lundborg (1999).

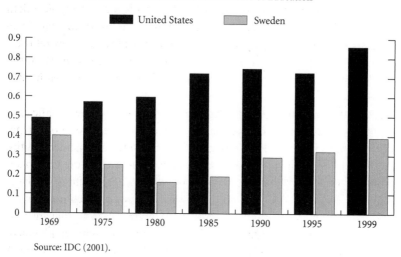

Figure 22. University Wage Premium: Percentage Difference in Average Wage Between Workers with 16 and 12 Years of Education

Source: IDC (2001).

lower, but steady source of income. With relative wages broadly stable for a long period, the incentive effects of wage compression on effective labor supply acquire a great deal of permanence.

Active Labor Market Programs

Sweden supplements passive labor market measures with a wide array of active labor market programs (ALMPs) that provide support conditional on some labor activity by the recipient. Programs of this kind in Sweden consist of self-employment grants, subsidized on-the-job training, wage and employment subsidies, and training courses. About 4.5 percent of the labor force participated in ALMPs in 1997. Sweden led the OECD rankings in the proportion of total labor market program spending allocated to ALMPs in the 1980s, and has remained among the top three since then. By specifically aiming to enhance employment rather than finance spells of unemployment, ALMPs, if well-designed, tend to alleviate structural rigidities, and help maintain attachment to the labor market, factors generally deemed crucial in bringing about a rebound in participation rates following major deteriorations in labor market conditions.[49] ALMPs do

---

[49]See, for instance, Forslund and Kolm (2000).

have costs for the budget, however, and may have an adverse effect on search behavior (since participants are likely to stop searching upon entering a program). In addition, with spending on ALMPs being less countercyclical than passive spending (OECD, 2000), they tend to reduce the automatic stabilizing effect associated with spending on unemployment. ALMPs also favorably affect the measured unemployment rate, because participants in ALMPs—other than in education programs—are not considered unemployed in official Swedish statistics.

Recent research points to the need for refinements to enhance the efficiency of ALMPs.[50] Measures to improve the intensity and efficiency of job searches hold the promise of raising employment in a cost-effective manner. Youths, the most mobile group in the labor force and with the greatest capacity to absorb risk, might often be better off if encouraged to keep searching for a job, especially because they have the most to lose from a prolonged cutoff from active employment. The most effective training programs are those that are close substitutes for regular employment. While this would argue for employment subsidies, the negative externality (crowding out) on others can be large. A sensible middle ground would be to target employment subsidies at the long-term unemployed, who are readily identified and would have little chance at reentering employment otherwise. Direct measures to support regional mobility have been found generally to be ineffective.

Temporary and Part-Time Employment

The rapid spread of temporary and part-time work helped the Swedish labor market attain much-needed flexibility and contributed to high participation rates. Part-time workers account for one-fifth of the labor force; the share of those on temporary contracts is approaching one-sixth. The availability of part-time jobs helps by tapping a supply of individuals who are unable or unwilling to work full time. Temporary workers, on the other hand, are the first to be hired in an upswing and released in a downturn. The high level of cyclicality in their employment may be an important source of aggregate labor market flexibility.

Conclusions

The Swedish labor market has proven to be fairly efficient in the upswing following the crisis of the early 1990s, and resilient in the slowdown during

---

[50]Much of the work in this area is by the Office for Labor Market Policy Evaluation (IFAU). See also Calmfors, Forslung, and Henström (2001).

2001–02. Participation rates and employment have increased, and are high relative to those in other OECD countries, although not compared with Swedish levels in the 1980s. Centralized bargaining, complemented by considerable local autonomy in setting relative wages, managed to constrain wage increases to a rate commensurate with productivity gains until the slowdown from mid-2001. However, the recent cyclical downturn in productivity is likely to pose a challenge to the ability of Swedish wage bargaining to deliver wage restraint on a macroeconomic level. The compressed wage scale, together with the tax transfer system, is likely to impair labor market efficiency and flexibility. On the other hand, extensive active labor market programs, the growing share of temporary and part-time work, and some reforms in the transfer system appear to largely offset these effects, as demonstrated by Sweden's consistently high employment and participation rates.

6   Investment and Savings

Taxes on investment and savings are among the key routes through which government may affect long-run growth and the efficiency of the intertemporal allocation of resources. In a closed economy, savings and investment are identical, so that policy measures that affect one would affect the other equally. Thus, the distinction between taxes at the corporate level and on personal savings would be of no economic significance. By contrast, in an economy open to capital movement, savings and investment are not identical, and the tax system may affect them differently.[51] This distinction is especially important in Sweden, with over 40 percent of the equity market being held by nonresidents. Indeed, the importance of the distinction has been appreciated in Sweden longer than in most other countries, with a traditional pattern—dating back to the days of "capitalism without capitalists"—of relatively low tax rates on corporate income combined with relatively high rates on saving. Even with a corporate rate of 57 percent at the start of the 1980s, for instance, the real impact of the tax on businesses was moderated by the investment funds system[52] and other provisions. As a result, the proportion of corporate profits taken in tax has for long often been less than half the statutory rate.[53] This chapter considers the current state of tax incentives to invest and save in Sweden.

---

[51]Empirically, savings and investment have been somewhat more closely correlated than might have been expected, a puzzle first noted by Feldstein and Horioka (1980). This underscores the importance of analyzing the impact of taxation on both.

[52]Under which firms could allocate up to half of their before-tax profits to an investment fund (escaping corporation tax on this amount), at the price of making a non-interest-bearing deposit at the Riksbank of some fraction of the amount reserved. The funds could then be used to finance investment in times of recession: in effect, such investment received immediate expensing. The scheme was abolished as part of the 1991 reform. See Södersten (1993) for an analysis of the impact of the system on incentives to invest.

[53]See Figure 4.1 of Agell, Englund, and Södersten (1998).

Investment

By altering the user cost of capital, taxes directly impact the incentive to invest. Empirical evidence increasingly confirms the potential importance of this effect. One recent survey of U.S. evidence, for instance, concludes that the elasticity of the capital stock with respect to the user cost is about –0.25 (Chirinko, Fazzari, and Meyer, 1999). Taxes clearly matter.

The central ingredient in assessing incentives to invest is the treatment of business income under the corporate tax. For foreign investors, the impact of this will then be modified by double taxation arrangements and the treatment of final investors in their residence countries. For Swedish investors, it will be mitigated by the Swedish personal tax system, discussed below. In either case, however, the corporate tax system is clearly critical.

Sweden has a relatively simple corporate tax system, with the 1991 reform establishing a rate of 28 percent and essentially standard depreciation allowances. The only significant nonstandard feature is a provision enabling firms to deduct up to 25 percent of their profits for allocation to a "periodization reserve," these funds to be recovered (and taxed) within no more than five years. This enables firms to defer part of their corporation tax liability: at an interest rate of 10 percent, it is equivalent to a reduction in the statutory rate from 28 to about 25 percent for the current tax year.

The net impact of the corporate tax system—both the statutory rate and the various allowances—is conveniently summarized by the marginal effective corporate tax rate (MECT). The MECT is defined as the difference between the before-tax return on a hypothetical marginal investment—that is, one that generates returns to the firm just adequate to meet its costs—and the rate of return net of corporation tax. (The various effective tax rate concepts used in this chapter, and the relationship between them, are spelled out in the Appendix.) The important benchmark here is a MECT of zero, meaning that the corporate tax system leaves marginal investment decisions entirely unaffected. This will be the case if the tax system enables all true costs associated with an investment, both financial and the acquisition cost of the asset, to be fully deducted over the life of the project. There are many ways in which this can be done. One is by allowing interest costs to be fully deductible against tax (as they are in Sweden) and grant depreciation allowances on physical assets that match the true reduction in their value from economic depreciation. Another is by adopting an "R-based cash flow" corporate tax under which all investment expenditure is immediately deductible against corporation tax, but interest payments are not.

One set of estimates of current MECTs for various kinds of investment in Sweden and under varying assumptions on the inflation rate, which affects the

Table 11. Marginal Effective Corporate Tax Rates (MECTs) in Sweden, 2001

	Inflation Rate (in percent)		
	0	2	5
Asset			
Machinery	−4.8	−6.3	−8.6
Buildings	7.8	5.9	2.4
Inventories	10.7	12.6	15.5
Source of finance			
Debt	−7.9	−10.7	−15.1
Equity	18.2	20.4	23.2
Overall	4.7	4.2	3.2

Source: Unpublished estimates by Jan Södersten.

real value of nominal interest deductions and depreciation reductions based on historic cost, is reported in Table 11. At Sweden's current inflation rate target of 2 percent, the MECT—averaged over all investments—is a little over 4 percent, so that the corporate tax system, considered in isolation, provides a modest discouragement to investment. As has been traditional in Sweden, the corporate tax bears relatively lightly on marginal investments. Within this, however, there is significant variation across types of investment. In particular, the low average reflects the balance between a significant subsidy to debt-financed investments, and an even larger charge on equity-financed investments. This is because the interest costs of debt finance are deductible against corporate tax, while the cost of servicing equity investments is not. There is also some distortion across forms of investment, with machinery being subsidized while inventories and, to a lesser extent, buildings carry a significant burden. The European Commission (2001) reaches similar conclusions as to the relative treatment of different kinds of investment, but finds a wider dispersion of MECTs around a higher mean, putting the average MECT at about 14 percent. These differences reflect the sensitivity of MECT calculations to relatively small changes in the underlying assumptions (for example, in the weights attached to different investments), and a reminder that not too much significance should be attached to precise figures. What does seem to emerge clearly from these calculations is that the corporate tax system in Sweden somewhat discourages investment on average, but with debt finance favored both in absolute terms (relative to a no-tax world) and relative to equity finance.

These estimates may overstate the distortion to investment decisions, however, to the extent that legal constraints on dividend distributions are binding. It is assumed in these calculations that the firm makes full use of all allowances available to it. In practice, however, it has long been a puzzle in Sweden that tax allowances are not fully utilized. Södersten (1993) cites evidence that in 1979–85 about two-thirds of tax allowances remained unused. One explanation for this is that after-tax profits constrain dividend payouts, so that the full use of allowances (depressing accounting profits by increasing stated depreciation) may imply an unwanted reduction in dividend payments. But if this constraint binds, then it can be shown—see Kanniainen and Södersten (1994) and Sørensen (1995)—that the corporate tax is effectively neutral, implying a MECT of zero.[54]

By international standards, Swedish MECTs are low. For comparison, Table 12 reports MECTs (for investments in different assets) for a range of countries. While the two sets of figures are calculated under different assumptions, and so not entirely comparable, it is clear that the corporate-level incentives to invest in Sweden are relatively strong. The same broad conclusion emerges from the European Commission study referred to above: across the EU, only Ireland and Italy have a lower average MECT.

In choosing a country in which to locate a discrete project, however, it is not simply the tax treatment of the marginal investment that matters, but also that of intramarginal investments (meaning those that yield more than the required after-tax return). For example, if all countries had a corporate tax with interest deductibility and true economic depreciation then—since any such tax is neutral—the MECT would be zero in all of them, even if they set different statutory rates. But firms will clearly wish, all else being equal, to locate investments in the country with the lowest statutory tax rate. For inter-

---

[54]If all after-tax profits are distributed then, from the identity between the firm's sources and uses of funds, investment must be financed from debt issues and the tax value of depreciation allowances. Thus, in the absence of a new equity issue, the equity part of the investment is identical to tax depreciation, that is, the cost of equity finance is effectively deductible against tax, implying neutrality. To see this more formally, write the identity between the firm's sources and uses of funds as:

$$\Pi + \Delta B = D + I + RB + \tau(\Pi - RB - D^T), \tag{6.1}$$

where D denotes dividends, Π profits, I investment, B debt, R the interest rate, τ the rate of corporation tax, and D^T depreciation for tax purposes. (For brevity, we ignore the possibility of new equity finance.) Suppose now that the firm is constrained not to pay dividends in excess of after-tax profits, so that:

$$D \leq (1 - \tau)(\Pi - RB - D^T). \tag{6.2}$$

If this constraint bites then, combining (6.1) and (6.2), $I = \Delta B + D^T$. Substituting from this for D^T in (6.1) then gives:

$$D = (1 - \tau)(\Pi + \Delta B - I - RB).$$

The corporate tax thus becomes equivalent to a proportional tax on the firm's cash flow, and hence is nondistorting.

Table 12. Swedish MECTs in an International Perspective

	Sweden	United States	Japan	Germany[1]	United Kingdom	Denmark	Netherlands
Plant and machinery	−4.8	4.0	18.0	6.0	6.0	3.0	7.0
Buildings	7.8	39.0	34.0	50.0	20.0	18.0	21.0

Sources: Jan Södersten; and Tables 3 and 4 of Bond and Chennells (2000).
[1]After completion of phased 2000 reform.

nationally mobile investments, the average effective corporate tax rate (AECT)—the proportion of the return on an investment that is taken in tax—also matters. All else being equal, investments will locate where the AECT is lowest. The AECT depends, like the MECT, on the detailed tax treatment of depreciation and financial costs. But in this case a more central role is played by the simple statutory rate of tax: if the corporate tax bears only on rents, for instance—so that the MECT is zero—the average effective tax rate coincides with the statutory rate.

Table 13 reports both the statutory rate of tax and the AECT (for a project earning a before-tax return of 20 percent) for the members of the EU. At around 32 percent, the AECT is lower in Sweden than in any other member state except Ireland, reflecting the combination of a structure that is not far from neutral and a low statutory rate.

The statutory rate has a further key role to play besides its impact on the marginal and average cost of real investment decisions. This is in relation to transfer pricing decisions and multinationals' choice of financing methods. The attractions of moving paper profits into Sweden either by manipulating the prices of intragroup financial or other transactions will depend on the differences between the statutory tax rate in Sweden and those faced elsewhere in the group. While there is little direct evidence of the impact of transfer pricing and similar arrangements on Sweden, the relatively low rate will clearly have tended to protect the Swedish tax base. Things may be changing, however. At the time of its introduction in 1991, the 28 percent rate was very low by international standards (as can be seen from Table 4 in Chapter 2); however, this is no longer the case.

Looking back, Sweden has indeed been successful in attracting foreign investment. In 1999, it was the third largest recipient of investment capital in the world; relative to GDP, it was the largest. While this mainly reflected two unusually large transactions, it seems plausible to suppose that the tax regime has been a broadly helpful factor. But corporate tax rates have since fallen sub-

Table 13. Statutory and Average Effective Corporate Tax Rates (AECTs) in the EU

	Statutory Rate of Corporation Tax[1]	AECT[2]
Austria	34.0	38.4
Belgium	40.2	44.5
Denmark	32.0	36.8
Finland	28.0	32.4
France	40.0	47.5
Germany	52.35	57.7
Greece	40.0	43.3
Ireland	10.0	13.0
Italy	41.25	34.0
Luxembourg	37.45	38.3
Netherlands	35.0	40.0
Portugal	37.4	42.0
Spain	35.0	40.0
Sweden	**28.0**	**31.0**
United Kingdom	30.0	35.7

[1]Including surcharges and average local taxes.
[2]Assuming a before-tax return of 20 percent, and calculated from Table 7 of European Commission (2001) as $AECT = \tau + (MECT)(1 - \tau)C / (0.2)$, where τ is the statutory rate of tax and C the user cost of capital. See the Appendix.

stantially in other countries, and (as discussed in Chapter 7) further downward pressures may emerge.

Savings

Studies of aggregate saving behavior generally find relatively low responsiveness to net rates of return, and hence to the tax treatment of savings. This does not mean, however, that tax effects are unimportant. As with labor supply, it is the substitution effect related to savings—in this case between present and future consumption—that determines the excess burden of the tax, and this can be substantial even if the uncompensated elasticity is low. Moreover, there is increasing evidence that taxation may distort the allocation of savings across different types of assets and, not least, its allocation across countries. The tax treatment of savings thus merits close attention.

The final after-tax return that Swedish investors receive from underlying real investments located in Sweden depends on both the treatment of the return on that investment at the business level, discussed in the previous section, and on the personal tax treatment of capital income. Under the dual form of income tax adopted in 1991, essentially all forms of such income—including dividend, interest, and capital gains—are taxed at a flat rate of 30 percent. Net returns are further reduced by the wealth tax, levied at 1.5 percent.

Marginal effective personal savings tax rates (MESTs)—showing the combined effect of business and ownership-level taxes—are high in Sweden. Such MESTs—reflecting the effect of investor-level taxes combined with the MECT discussed above—are reported in Table 14. The MEST varies across ownership class, naturally being lower for tax-exempt institutional shareholders and insurance companies than for persons. For the latter, at an inflation rate of 2 percent, the MEST is about 45 percent, far higher than the average MECT of around 4 percent (see Table 11). Indeed, the extent to which the MEST exceeds the MECT—by over 40 points—may at first seem strange given the flat tax on capital income of 30 percent. Part of the explanation is that nonlinearities arising from their interaction mean that the combined effects of corporate and personal taxation are not simply the product of each taken in isolation.[55] Perhaps more important, the reported MESTs also reflect the impact of the wealth tax and can be interpreted as showing that its effect can be substantial. At a nominal interest rate of 10 percent, for instance, a 1.5 percent tax rate on wealth is equivalent to a tax of 15 percent on the associated annualized income.

Around this high average level of the marginal effective taxation of savings, there is considerable variation between different sources of finance. Debt is by far the cheapest source of finance, followed by retained earnings, a ranking that reflects the deductibility of interest payments but not of financing equity returns. Most heavily taxed is new equity finance. This reflects the "classical" form of corporation tax in place in Sweden, with dividends being taxed at the personal level without any credit or deduction being given against corporate tax. Funds injected into companies in the form of new equity are thus subject to double taxation, tax being payable both at the corporate level from the income generated and at the personal level on the payment of these proceeds as dividends. For equity finance in the form of retained profits, in contrast, the personal tax treatment of dividends is irrelevant. (For retained earnings, the choice is between distributing profits today or, instead, reinvesting them and paying dividend taxes in the future; so long as its rate does not change over time, the dividend tax cancels out of the calculation.)

The double taxation of dividends discourages the use of new equity finance, which may cause particular difficulties for new firms traditionally re-

---

[55]One might naturally suppose that (and it would certainly be convenient if) the MEST could be decomposed into distinct effects from corporate and personal taxation, along the lines $1 - MEST = (1 - MECT)(1 - MEPT)$, where $MECT$ is as defined in the previous section, and so depends only on corporate tax parameters, while $MEPT$ is a marginal effective personal income tax rate that depends only on personal tax parameters. As discussed in the Appendix, however, it turns out that—because the user cost of capital generally depends on both corporate and personal tax parameters—this is not in general possible.

Table 14. Marginal Effective Personal Savings Tax Rates (MESTs) in Sweden, 2001

	Inflation Rate (in percent)		
	0	2	5
Asset			
Machinery	17.3	19.0	21.5
Buildings	28.1	29.4	31.0
Inventories	30.3	35.1	42.2
Source of finance			
Debt	13.6	15.1	17.0
New share issues	46.6	52.5	61.2
Retained earnings	37.3	41.2	46.8
Owner			
Households	40.7	45.3	51.9
Tax-exempt[1]	8.1	8.4	8.6
Insurance company	23.5	27.0	32.0
Overall	25.4	28.0	31.7

Source: Unpublished estimates by Jan Södersten.
[1]The figures reflect the payment of taxes at corporate level (e.g., by pension funds).

liant on this as a major source of finance. It may also give rise to significant international tax planning opportunities. For example, it has been said that in a merger of Swedish and Finnish banks it became tax advantageous to locate the headquarters of the new enterprise in Finland rather than Sweden. Since Finland operates a partial imputation system, under which Finnish shareholders can use part of the corporate tax paid in the country to offset their personal tax liability, they prefer, all else being equal, to receive dividends from a company resident in Finland.

While the difficulties associated with the double taxation of dividends are clear—and have been worsened by developments over the 1990s[56]—there is little evidence as to how costly they are. There are few estimates for Sweden—or indeed anywhere else—of the welfare cost of the distortion in financing methods it implies, especially for new enterprises. Moreover, it can be argued that in an economy as open as Sweden the effect will be largely mitigated.[57] For if the

---

[56]As noted in Chapter 2, the logic of the dual income tax suggests that dividends not be taxed if corporate income is taxed at the rate applied to other forms of capital income. The 1991 reform went a long way in this direction: although dividends were fully taxable, the impact of this on the cost of new equity finance was mitigated by allowing firms to claim a partial deduction in respect of new equity issues (the "Annell deduction"). In January 1994 both the tax on dividends and the Annell deduction were removed. But when the dividend tax was later reintroduced by a new government in 1995, the Annell deduction was not.

[57]This point is made by Boadway and Bruce (1992) and developed further by Devereux and Freeman (1995).

marginal purchaser of new shares is a foreigner (a plausible supposition for large Swedish companies), then the domestic tax on dividends should have no effect on incentives to invest or even on share prices (because it applies only to residents). The effect may be more marked for smaller companies unlikely to be purchased directly by foreign investors (who are less well-informed as to their prospects). As Apel and Södersten (1999) point out, even then the effects of double dividend taxation may be reduced by the presence of foreign investors: since foreign investors do not pay the dividend tax, they will have a comparative advantage in holding the traded shares, bidding up their price and hence inducing domestic shareholders to substitute towards nontraded shares. This would tend to lower the cost of funds for unlisted companies. Measures have been taken, in any event, to mitigate the effects of the dividend tax for such companies.[58]

There has been continuing controversy as to whether Sweden would benefit by moving to some alternative structure that removes or further mitigates the double taxation of dividends. There are a number of ways in which this might be done. Sweden might, for instance, adopt some form of imputation system, of the kind currently in place in Finland, France, Norway, Australia, and elsewhere. This, however, would run counter to a recent trend away from imputation within the EU. Complications and potential legal difficulties associated with international aspects of imputation[59] have been a key reason for recent decisions to shift from imputation and towards classical taxation in Germany, Ireland, Italy, and the United Kingdom. There are alternatives: a credit in relation to dividends paid to residents might be given at the corporate rather than personal level;[60] or, simpler still, dividends might be exempted from personal tax. Such measures are unlikely to be especially costly in revenue terms. While there is no strong evidence that the double taxation of dividends currently causes significant welfare losses, it raises limited revenue, and there is also no reason to suppose that it conveys great benefit.[61] A case can

---

[58]Distributions to individual shareholders by unlisted or nonresident companies (having or having had no substantial ownership of listed companies) are exempt to the extent of an imputed return on invested equity.

[59]They arise, for example, from the natural inclination to deny imputation credit on dividends paid from foreign-source income that has not borne tax in the home country; and legal requirements in the EU may require that the credit be extended to residents of all member states, potentially eroding the revenue collected at corporate level.

[60]See Muten (1995).

[61]Fuest and Huber (2000) argue for the double taxation of dividends in a small economy open to capital movements on the grounds that doing otherwise amounts to an inappropriate subsidy to domestic asset holding. Against this would need to be set, however, the costs of distorting the financing decisions of firms without access to international capital markets.

thus be made for further reducing the tax burden on dividends, not least in terms of the internal logic of the dual income tax. Nevertheless, the international trend in recent years has been toward, rather than away from, the current Swedish approach. Opinions differ on whether or not this has been desirable—perhaps it would have been better for EU members to extend imputation credits routinely to residents of other member states rather than move to double taxation—but these trends do mean that further reducing the tax on dividends would be seen as a bold step.

The calculations reported above concern investment in real business assets. Traditionally, and like many others, the Swedish tax system has treated relatively more favorably investment in owner-occupied housing, which benefits from the combination of interest deductibility and exemption of the effective return. While the 1991 reform, and others in the late 1980s, substantially reduced the tax advantages of owner occupation[62]—by limiting interest deductibility, replacing a tax on imputed income with a more burdensome real estate tax, and extending VAT to housing construction costs—some preference seems likely to remain. A particular concern with this is that the tax advantages to owner occupation may worsen the bias against the provision of rental properties that is implied by the continuing de facto rent control in Sweden.

The recent increase in valuations for the property tax—which had been frozen for several years—led to substantial pressure to lighten the burden of the tax. This was in part on distributional grounds, with less well-off residents of sought-after holiday home areas facing awkward tax bills. In the event, the government announced in August 2001 its intention to cut the rate of real estate tax from 1.2 to 1 percent. Property tax rates have indeed been rather high by EU standards (though revenues have not, as can be seen from Table 3 in Chapter 2). Nevertheless, the real estate tax has important merits: in so far as it bears on the immobile attractions of the location itself, it is likely to impose a relatively modest marginal excess burden. Further erosion of the tax should thus be avoided.

The Swedish real estate tax has the striking feature—very unusual outside the Nordic countries—of being allocated to central government. The usual argument is that property taxes are well suited as a transparent means of local finance, being in some respects akin to a benefit tax. One merit of its allocation to the center, however, is the prospect of avoiding downward tax competition, an attraction that should be exploited in light of the emerging pressures on tax revenues in the coming years.

---

[62]See Chapter 3 of Agell, Englund, and Södersten (1998).

Coherent policymaking in the housing sector requires a long overdue review and reform of all interventions in the area, embracing taxes, regulation, and the housing assistance system. The potential efficiency costs in such a key area, with considerable implications for the functioning of the labor market and the allocation of capital, are substantial. In particular, labor market mobility could be substantially improved by eliminating de facto rent control in large cities, which would facilitate a reduction in shortages of dwellings in areas where labor demand is high.

The wealth tax also merits significant reform. Levied at the relatively high rate of 1.5 percent above the relatively modest threshold of SKr 1.5 million (for a married couple), it can imply a significant disincentive to saving, as noted earlier. Even relatively modest housing wealth, for instance, is likely to incur a charge. At the same time, however, the tax is marked by exclusions that are likely to favor the most well-off: in particular, most unlisted shares are excluded, as are principal shareholdings (over 25 percent of voting rights). Since it is relatively easy for the well-advised to structure their affairs so as to take advantage of such provisions, the fairness of the tax is undermined. There are two main options for reform. One is to simply abolish the tax, which raised only around SKr 6 billion in 1999, about 0.5 percent of total tax revenue. As can be seen from the international comparison of tax rates in Table 4 (Chapter 2), many countries have no wealth tax, and those that do commonly set a lower rate and higher threshold than does Sweden. There seems, however, to be general support in Sweden for the existence of a tax on wealth. This points towards the second option, which is to mitigate its disincentive effects and improve its fairness by further increasing the threshold and scaling back exemptions. While many wealthy individuals will doubtless find other ways to avoid the tax, the remaining distortions may be a price worth paying for the equity gain from the tax.

Conclusions

Sweden has long perceived itself as an open economy in terms of investment flows and has sought to encourage investment more generally. Consistent with this, marginal effective tax rates have traditionally been relatively low by international standards. Average effective rates, too, have been moderate. With the adoption of the dual income tax at the start of the 1990s, Sweden opted for the pragmatic view that a flat tax at a low rate could be more effective in taxing capital income than attempting to tax it at progressive nominal rates. The question, to which we turn later, is whether even such modest rates will prove sustainable in the years ahead.

7 Redistribution

A key objective of the Swedish welfare state is to ensure a distribution of real income and a pattern of economic opportunities that meet criteria of social justice with broad political support. A wide range of policy instruments are deployed to this end, including:

- Regulations and other interventions aimed at fostering labor market incomes of the lower-paid, including a tradition of wage compression and support of work-related expenditures, notably childcare;

- A progressive tax system, intended to ensure that the burden of financing public expenditure bears disproportionately on the better-off (in the sense that they face a higher average tax rate);

- Public and largely uniform provision of key commodities, notably health care and education, serving both as a direct instrument of redistribution—to the extent that their value is independent of income, their effect is akin to reducing tax payments by the same absolute amount, so increasing progressivity—and as a means of promoting greater long-term equality by equalizing earnings capacities; and

- An extensive system of direct income transfers (the main ones are described in Box 1 in Chapter 2).

Though not necessarily the most important element in this set of redistributive measures, the transfer system has naturally received particular attention. As shown in Table 2 (Chapter 2), income transfers to households currently amount to over 18 percent of GDP, significantly above the OECD average and matched among the most developed countries only by Austria, Germany, and France. This chapter considers how well this transfer system has performed in terms of its primary objective of reducing inequality and alleviating poverty.

Inequality and Poverty

In terms of standard indicators, the outcomes for inequity and poverty in Sweden are as egalitarian as in virtually any other country. Table 15 reports recent comparative statistics for EU countries. As a simple summary indicator of inequality, the first column shows the share of equivalized disposable income—income after all taxes and transfers adjusted for family size and composition—earned by the top quintile relative to that of the bottom quintile. The greater this ratio, the more unequal[63] is the distribution of disposable income. At 3.7, this ratio is far below the average of 5.2; only Denmark has a more egalitarian outcome in this sense. The poverty outcome is also impressive. The second column reports the headcount measure of poverty—the proportion of the population that is in relative poverty (after taxes and transfers)—when the poverty-line level of income is taken to be 60 percent of the median.[64] The outcome in Sweden is again far better than the average: 14 percent of the population remains in poverty, compared with an average of 17.2 percent elsewhere in the EU. While different choices for the poverty line can in principle give somewhat different impressions of cross-country performance, Jäntti and Danziger (2000) show that on a test of first-order poverty dominance—the requirement that the headcount measure of poverty be lower for any choice of poverty line—only a few countries (notably Austria, Finland, and Germany) fare better, while many fare unambiguously worse.

There are many other and perhaps better ways of measuring inequality and poverty. The headcount measure takes no account, for instance, of the depth of the poverty of those below the cutoff poverty line. Yet most summary measures convey much the same impression. For instance, Gottschalk and Smeeding (2000) report Sweden as having the second-lowest after-tax and transfer Gini coefficient among 21 developed countries (only Finland has a lower one), while Jäntti and Danziger (2000) find that in terms of second-order poverty dominance—looking not at the numbers in poverty for any given poverty line but the extent to which incomes fall short of that line—Sweden's performance remains relatively good.

---

[63]This statement is loose: a higher value for this ratio does not imply the Lorenz dominance usually regarded as necessary and sufficient for unambiguous inequality statements.

[64]This thus corresponds to a relative notion of poverty. The high average living standards in Sweden and low headcount ratio relative to the median imply, of course, low absolute poverty.

Table 15. After-Tax/Transfer Inequality and Poverty in the EU, 1996

	Inequality[1]	Poverty[2]
Austria	4.0	13.0
Denmark	2.9	11.0
France	4.5	16.0
Germany	4.7	16.0
Greece	6.1	21.0
Ireland	5.6	18.0
Italy	6.0	19.0
Luxembourg	4.5	12.0
Netherlands	4.7	12.0
Portugal	6.6	20.0
Spain	5.9	18.0
Sweden	3.7	14.0
United Kingdom	5.6	19.0
EU15	5.2	17.2

Source: Eurostat.
[1]Ratio of total equivalized disposable income of top and bottom quintiles.
[2]Percent of population with equivalized after-transfer income below 60 percent of median.

More fundamentally, in focusing on the pattern of annual incomes, these summary measures make no distinction between transitory and permanent differences in economic position. A more complete treatment would focus on differences in lifetime economic status. It may be, for instance, that greater inequality of annual income in one society relative to another simply reflects a greater variance (around the same mean) of incomes over the lifetime; a difference that, if capital markets enable individuals to borrow freely against future income, is of little significance to economic well-being. In a similar spirit, a given incidence of poverty may be viewed as less damaging if those in poverty in different years tend to be different people. While data problems pose difficulty for lifetime assessments of inequality and poverty,[65] such evidence as there is suggests that in this dimension, too, Sweden performs well. Jäntti and Danziger (2000) report exit rates from poverty as being relatively high in Sweden (bettered, within a set of 10 industrial countries, only by Finland and the Netherlands). Intergenerational mobility in Sweden also appears relatively high. Indeed, comparing with Swedish immigrants to the United

[65]To the extent that individuals' consumption decisions reflect their own assessment of their lifetime income prospects, the distribution of consumption would provide a better indicator of lifetime inequality than that of relatively short-term income measures. But no comparative data of this sort appear to be available.

States, Björklund and Jäntti (1997) find the correlation between earnings of fathers and sons to be far lower in Sweden than in the United States.

Impact of Policy on Inequality and Poverty

Determining how far low levels of inequality and poverty in Sweden reflect policy requires, in principle, constructing the counterfactual of how real income would be distributed in the absence of policy interventions. While it is natural to take as a starting point the actual distribution of income before taxes and transfers, that will itself reflect the incentive effects created by the tax and transfer system. The assurance of a pension, for instance, may reduce the earnings of those approaching retirement. These responses are likely to mean, for example, that poverty in the absence of policy would be less than poverty measured simply in terms of the before-tax and transfer incomes that are actually received in the presence of the tax transfer system.[66]

Considerable effort has traditionally been made in Sweden to equalize the distribution of gross earnings by compressing wages and promoting employment of the low-skilled, so that a simple comparison of incomes before and after the effects of the tax transfer system may understate the extent of redistribution achieved by policy. As seen in Chapter 5, wage dispersion has been relatively low in Sweden: in 1993, the wage rate of the highest paid decile was about 59 percent above the median, about the same as in Germany, but much lower than in the United Kingdom (86 percent) and France (99 percent). The impact of this on the distribution of earnings has been amplified by traditionally high levels of employment. Moreover, it seems that this relatively egalitarian distribution of earnings cannot easily be explained in terms of an underlying homogeneity of abilities. Björklund and Freeman (1997), for instance, find that the earnings distribution of Swedes in the United States is essentially the same as the overall U.S. distribution. Thus the relative equality of earnings in Sweden appears to be largely attributable to policy operating outside the tax transfer system, so that much redistribution has already been done before this comes into play.

The immediate redistributive effect of the tax transfer system—meaning simply the difference between the inequality of market incomes and that of disposable incomes—is easier to assess. And it has clearly been considerable. Table

---

[66]The impact of the tax transfer system on before-tax inequality is less clear-cut. If the main impact of progressivity is to induce the higher-paid to earn less, the effect of policy will be to reduce before-tax inequality; on the other hand, the inducement to risk taking implied by social insurance may generate increased before-tax inequality.

Table 16. Gini Coefficients and Redistribution

	Before-Tax Factor Income	Disposable Income	Proportionate Reduction (in percent)
1975	0.476	0.233	51.1
1980	0.476	0.206	56.7
1985	0.495	0.221	55.4
1990	0.501	0.246	50.9
1995	0.563	0.256	54.5
1999	0.578	0.294	49.1

Source: Table 57, *Income Distribution Survey in 1999* (Statistics Sweden).

16 shows that the tax transfer system has for many years reduced the extent of inequality in annual income by 50 to 55 percent. This is a very considerable amount: the comparable figure has been around 35 percent in Germany, for instance, and 25 percent in the United States.[67] In terms of poverty reduction, Jäntti and Danziger (2000) find that around the start of the 1990s, Sweden was one of only 3 of 15 industrial countries in which the tax transfer system reduced the headcount measure of poverty (relative to a poverty line of 50 percent of median income) by over 75 percent.

Within a broadly constant total extent of tax transfer redistribution, however, there has been a significant change in the relative contribution of taxes and spending. With the 1991 reform, the tax system has become significantly less progressive, as illustrated in Table 10 (Chapter 5) and Table 16. The effect of this on the overall distribution of income has been largely offset, however, by increased redistribution on the spending side. In particular, the increase in child allowances has targeted a group generally poor in terms of market income, and the increase in housing allowances has been directly targeted at low-income households with children. Thus, the net effect of the reforms of the early 1990s has been to leave the overall extent of redistribution broadly unaffected, but with a significant change in its pattern: roughly speaking, redistribution between those with and without children has increased, while within household types it has, if anything, fallen.

Much redistribution is intertemporal rather than interpersonal. Table 17 shows the broad composition of transfers to households, with the significant role of child and housing allowances—over 10 percent of the total—apparent. Almost half of all transfers, however, are in the form of pensions. The importance of these transfers—reflected in what are by international standards particularly low poverty rates among children and the elderly (Jäntti and

---

[67]See Table 13 of OECD (2000).

Table 17. Transfers to Households
(In percent of GDP)

Total	19.1
Of which	
Pensions	9.0
Sickness	4.2
Unemployment benefits	2.0
Child benefits	2.0
Student benefits	0.6
Housing and social allowances	1.3

Danziger, 2000)—again points to the importance of taking a lifetime perspective on redistribution. To the extent that pensions are related to contributions, they reflect not redistribution across persons but redistribution over the life cycle. Indeed the same may be true to a large extent of child allowances. Thus one estimate is that about two-thirds of all transfers in Sweden are intertemporal rather than interpersonal (OECD, 2000, p. 116). This is not to say that such redistribution is without value. To the extent that market imperfections mean that individuals are unable themselves to borrow against their future incomes, state intervention may be welfare enhancing. The argument is likely to be less powerful in Sweden than elsewhere, however, since capital markets are well developed. Moreover, the evidence suggests that relatively few Swedish households are liquidity constrained, and any benefits in overcoming market failure must be set against the distortions that arise if the extent of forced saving exceeds the level individuals would wish to undertake.

Nevertheless, empirical evidence suggests that the extent of interpersonal redistribution achieved is considerable. Following a set of individuals from 1971 to 1991, Björklund and Jäntti (1997) find that the extent of redistribution of lifetime incomes through the tax system is broadly matched in magnitude by that of annual incomes among Swedish income earners.

A full assessment of the extent of redistribution would also take account of the public provision of various services at less than market value, which in Sweden is considerable. Many of these items—health care, education, and social services—are very extensive. They not only effectively redistribute purchasing power directly, and in ways that may have better incentive effects than cash redistribution,[68] but may also have a significant equalizing effect in terms

---

[68]The direct provision of private goods may weaken the self-selection constraints—preserving incentives for the more able—that limit the ability to redistribute through the tax system. See, for instance, Blackorby and Donaldson (1988).

of their long- and short-term implications for labor market status. Subsidized childcare, for example, has facilitated the high levels of labor market participation. Quantifying these effects is difficult, however, both conceptually (in the proper valuation of services enjoyed, for instance) and empirically (in terms of the required data on usage), since no thorough and internationally comparable figures appear to be available. The extent of such expenditures in Sweden suggests, however, that their joint effect is substantial.

Conclusions

There is no doubt that the Swedish welfare state has achieved a great deal in ensuring a distribution of real incomes in conformity with a broad egalitarian social consensus. Even one of its harshest critics has lauded this as "... a major achievement of modern civilization" (Lindbeck, 1993). The question is how these benefits weigh against the efficiency losses that, as described in previous chapters, have been incurred in pursuing these objectives, and whether the variety of pressures now looming threaten their preservation.

8   Pressures on the Welfare State

Whatever one thinks of its past performance, it is clear that the welfare state is likely to face significant challenges in the years ahead. Increasing internationalization of economic activity seems set to make it more difficult to raise revenue than it has been in the past,[69] and at the same time demographic change points towards significantly increased revenue needs. This chapter assesses the extent of the challenges, and their likely impact on the considerable public support that has underpinned extensive government intervention in Sweden.

Increased International Mobility of Tax Bases

There is widespread awareness that the increased internationalization of economic activity may alter the effectiveness of, and hence the proper extent and form of, government intervention, with the prospect of a continued increase in the mobility of tax bases reducing the tax rates that Sweden optimally imposes and the level of revenue it optimally collects.[70] Formal and informal obstacles to cross-border transactions in capital, commodities, and labor have been eased, and are likely to be eased still further in the future, both by policy measures—within the context of EU membership and more generally—and by advances in information technology that reduce informational imperfections and transaction costs. As a result, these cross-border transactions are likely to become more sensitive to cross-national tax differentials. This increased elasticity of the tax base with respect to tax rates then tends to reduce

---

[69]Concern at the potential significance of this trend toward globalization led the government to appoint a committee to review its potential implications.

[70]See Boije (2001) for a comprehensive overview of the tax policy challenges Sweden's welfare state faces and Tanzi (2000) for an overview of the general issues.

the level of tax rates that each country finds optimal to impose—and also to reduce the associated level of revenue that it is optimal to raise—by reducing the revenue raised from, and increasing the excess burden created by, a marginal increase in the tax rate.[71] More generally, increased mobility makes it harder to sustain taxes other than benefit taxes (those that finance offsetting benefits received by the taxpayer, whether a company or individual). This implies, in particular, that redistribution—the essence of which is to impose a net fiscal loss on some in order to convey a net fiscal benefit to others—may become harder. This effect will be amplified to the extent that the better-off receive forms of income that derive from more mobile sources.[72] These prospective problems are not unique to Sweden, of course[73]—being faced, in particular, by many other EU members[74]—but the extensive reliance on government intervention makes Sweden a key case study for others interested in how they, too, might be affected by these developments.

While the general proposition that increased internationalization will put downward pressure on tax revenues is clear enough, the quantitative extent of this effect is not. There remain various subtleties in assessing the impact of internationalization on the design of tax transfer systems. There are complex interactions, for example, between the effects of increased mobility of labor and capital. Increased mobility of labor may actually reduce the downward pressure on capital taxes, since the beneficial effect on wages of attracting more inward investment may be dissipated by the migration it induces (Kessler, Lülfesmann, and Meyers, 2000). Nevertheless, the key qualitative issues are

---

[71]There are exceptions, although these are unlikely to apply to Sweden. For instance, opening up the possibility to export a good in which a country has significant market power creates an incentive to set a high production or export tax to exploit that power.

[72]This is not to say, of course, that increased internationalization is undesirable, since other gains may well offset the fiscal difficulties posed. Openness allows countries to take advantage of technological innovations embedded in new capital goods from abroad; import competition can force domestic firms to operate more efficiently and raise the rate of innovation; and the opportunity to produce for export markets can allow the exploitation of economies of scale and scope in production. As for empirical evidence, several studies find a positive correlation between growth and exports (Balassa, 1978; Krueger, 1978; Bhagwati and Srinivasan, 1979; Otani and Villanueva, 1990).

[73]Nor are they unfamiliar to economists, the point being put eloquently by Adam Smith in his *Wealth of Nations* (1776): "The proprietor of stock is properly a citizen of the world, and is not necessarily attached to any particular county. He would be apt to abandon the country in which he was exposed to a vexatious inquisition, in order to be assessed a burdensome tax, and would remove his stock to some other country where he could either carry on his business, or enjoy his fortune more at ease. A tax which tended to drive away stock from any particular country, would so far tend to dry up every ounce of revenue, both to the sovereign and to the society."

[74]Sinn (2000 and 2002), for example, discusses the implications for Germany and the EU, respectively, focusing especially on issues of labor mobility.

broadly clear. Far less clear is their likely quantitative significance, and it is on this that the rest of this chapter focuses, taking in turn the three key broad tax bases: capital, commodities, and labor.

Capital

Sweden has long (and successfully) sought to maintain an attractive tax environment for inward investment, as discussed in Chapter 5. Mobility of real investment is nothing new for Sweden, which has for many years essentially viewed itself as an archetypal small open economy, open to capital movements and with little ability to influence the return that potential investors can earn in the world capital market.

It is quite a robust theoretical prescription that such an economy should not levy any source-based tax on the marginal return to investment.[75] For in a small open economy the effective incidence of such a tax cannot be on the owners of capital, since they will ensure that they receive in Sweden the same after-tax return that they can earn elsewhere. It can only be on domestic immobile factors—principally labor—but with the unwanted side effect of raising the gross return to capital and so inducing excessive labor intensity of production. Put differently, increased capital mobility increases the marginal excess burden associated with a source-based capital tax, an effect that Hansson (1987) shows to be potentially significant. This distortion can be avoided by simply taxing the immobile factors directly. Since the key source-based tax is the corporate tax, this prescription translates into that of a marginal effective corporate tax rate of zero. While Sweden has not fully eliminated source-based taxes on all marginal investments, it was seen in Chapter 5 that the average level of such taxes has been low for many years. Although there is scope for achieving this effect by simpler means—establishing more uniform treatment of different kinds of investments—there is little reason to suppose or recommend that this aspect of tax policy will or should change as internationalization intensifies.

The prescription of no source-based tax on marginal investments does not imply, however, that there should be no corporate tax, though there are strong reasons for setting it at an internationally competitive level. Without a business-level tax, tax could be avoided by incorporating, retaining earnings in the corporation, and delaying the realization of the consequent capital gains.[76]

---

[75]The result is an application of the Diamond-Mirrlees (1971) theorem on the desirability of production efficiency; an explicit statement is in Frenkel, Razin, and Yuen (1996).

[76]Even if the income is taxed when later taken out of the corporation, the delay in payment will have reduced its present value; in effect, the taxpayer would have received an interest-free loan from the government.

Moreover, a well-designed corporation tax can raise revenue by taxing the rents earned on intramarginal investments without distorting investment incentives at the margin. For investments from countries that give a credit for taxes paid in the source country—such as the United States, the main single proximate source of direct investment in Sweden—taxes can be levied up to the level of the residence-country tax without imposing any additional burden on the investor, the effect of the credit being that residence-country taxes are reduced one-for-one by source-country payments. The rate of corporation tax cannot be raised too far, however. Doing so will increase the average effective rate of corporation tax (a concept explained in Chapter 6 and the Appendix), even for investments from jurisdictions offering foreign tax credits, since no additional credit will be available once the rate in Sweden exceeds the residence-country rate, thereby making Sweden less attractive to foreign investors. Only rents specific to Sweden can be taxed at high rates without risk of driving investment away, and these are likely to become increasingly limited as the Swedish economy becomes more integrated with the rest of the EU and other countries. Not least, high statutory rates of corporation tax make a country vulnerable to transfer pricing and financial operations that shift paper profits to jurisdictions with lower taxes.

Current arrangements in Sweden appear quite well-adapted to these considerations. The rate of corporation tax is reasonably low by the standards of the major developed economies. Revenue from the corporation tax is somewhat below OECD and EU averages, but nevertheless remains quite substantial, at around 5.7 percent of total tax revenue in 1998, or 2.9 percent of GDP. Nor has there been any clear tendency for receipts to fall: in the latter part of the 1980s they were around 2 percent of GDP. This apparent resilience of corporate tax revenues relative to GDP has been observed in many other countries and is something of a puzzle (Devereux, Griffith, and Klemm, 2002). It reflects the consequences of reforms that, like the 1991 reform in Sweden, have lowered statutory rates of corporation tax (so minimizing the erosion of the base as a result of transfer pricing devices) while broadening the base (so bolstering revenue, at least from relatively immobile domestic investments). Nevertheless, continued downward pressure on the rate of corporation tax in Sweden can be expected. While the 28 percent statutory tax rate established in 1994 was then among the very lowest of developed economies, this is no longer the case. The U.K. rate, for instance, is now 30 percent; that in Germany was reduced dramatically by their 2000 reform from 40 percent (on undistributed profits) to 25 percent;[77] the Irish rate is to be reduced to 12.5

---

[77]Including local business taxes, however, the average is about 38 percent.

percent by 2005; and Estonia, a potential EU member, has no corporation tax at all.

The likely extent of these pressures on corporate tax revenues is hard to gauge, but, in the absence of effective international coordination, the direction is clear. With the MECT averaging close to zero, there is little prospect of painlessly replacing corporate taxes by an explicit increase in the tax on employment income. In this sense the whole of the corporate tax revenue is at stake. The pressures on these revenues would be mitigated to some degree if the EU were to adopt a minimum rate of corporation tax (as proposed, for example, by the Ruding Committee, 1992) or, perhaps, move towards some system of formula apportionment[78] (a possibility raised by the European Commission, 2001). These remain remote prospects, however, and in any event, pressures from low tax rates outside the EU would remain. Recent experience and Sweden's long-established expertise in preserving an attractive tax environment while sustaining revenues both imply a limited risk of a dramatic erosion of corporate tax revenues in the near future. But it would be prudent to factor in a modest reduction into medium-term fiscal planning.

In contrast, openness per se does not imply that taxes on personal savings are optimally zero. In Sweden, as is the norm, capital income accruing to individuals is taxed on a residence basis; that is, Swedish residents are liable to Swedish tax on their capital income (and, under the wealth tax, on their assets) wherever in the world it arises (generally with a credit for foreign taxes paid on that income). In sharp contrast to the result for source taxes referred to above, there is no intrinsic reason for a small open economy to set a low or zero residence-based tax. There may well be other arguments for doing so, in terms of the impact of savings on capital accumulation, or the structure of consumer preferences,[79] but openness as such does not directly affect the optimal tax treatment of personal savings. The real issue is simply the difficulty of enforcing the residence principle, given the opportunities—which are likely to continue to increase—that internationalization creates for individuals to locate their savings in low-tax jurisdictions and simply fail to report the associated income and/or capital to the authorities of their residence country. Evasion of domestic savings taxes by this route jeopardizes revenue and creates pressure to reduce the tax rates applied.

---

[78]Under such a system a multinational's total of earnings across a series of countries is allocated to each by reference to some formula proxying the extent of its activity in each. The "perhaps" in the text reflects the possibility that tax competition might actually be more intense under such a system (as argued by Keen, 1999; and Nielsen, Raimondos-Møller, and Schjelderup, 1999).

[79]See, for instance, King (1980) and Chamley (1986) and, for a brief survey of issues in the optimal taxation of capital income, Boadway and Keen (2002).

Though reliable information is naturally hard to obtain, the revenue loss from undeclared assets abroad is likely to be relatively small at present. There are few obstacles to Swedish residents investing abroad, as they have been able to legally acquire foreign equities since 1989 and to hold foreign bank accounts since 1993. Assessing the extent to which these opportunities are used to evade Swedish tax is, by the very nature of the activity, extremely difficult. The Social Democratic Party has produced estimates, based on the discrepancy between financial and national accounts, suggesting that households' undeclared savings abroad amounted to about SKr 350 billion in 1997.[80] This is equivalent to about 16 percent of the sector's total measured financial assets, and nearly double the corresponding level of estimated undeclared savings in 1992. Assuming that these assets earned an average return of 8 percent, and that they would be fully taxable in Sweden—so ignoring, for instance, any tax withheld for which a credit would be available in Sweden—the implied revenue loss is about SKr 8.4 billion, or around 0.8 percent of general government revenue in 1997. Assuming further that one-third of these assets were also liable to wealth taxes, the implied revenue loss is still less than 1 percent of total revenue.

While the revenue loss would rise if the extent of evasion were to increase, it is unlikely to be dramatic. Taking the extreme case to illustrate possible orders of magnitude, if all interest and dividend income that was taxed in Sweden in 1998 had instead arisen abroad and been undeclared, general government revenue would have been lower by about SKr 11.6 billion, or 1 percent of the total. Grossing up (using an assumed 10 percent return) and taking one-third of the implied asset base to be properly liable to wealth tax, the revenue loss rises to about 1.2 percent.[81] Since individuals are likely to continue to hold a substantial portion of their wealth in real estate and Swedish equities, the opportunities for evading individual taxes on wealth and capital gains by taking income abroad, though not zero, are likely to be less. If a third of the bases of each were to vanish due to underreporting, revenue would fall by an additional SKr 7.7 billion, for a total loss—from all three sources—of a little under 2 percent of general government revenues.

The illustrative calculations in the preceding paragraph are based on assumptions that will tend to overstate the revenue risk. In one important respect, however, they may understate it. In so far as interest income is deductible against Swedish tax at a marginal rate higher than that at which it is

---

[80]The ministry of finance has indicated that a subsequent revision of the national accounts is likely to reduce these figures.

[81]This is broadly consistent with the estimate of SKr 11 billion for 1999 reported in Table S40 of National Tax Board (2000).

taxed abroad, there are potential gains from pure tax arbitrage. Borrowing SKr 100 in Sweden at an interest rate of 10 percent in order to lend, at the same rate, in a country that taxes interest at 5 percent—a transaction that generates no profit in the absence of taxes—generates a profit after taxes of SKr 2.5 (the excess of the deduction in Sweden, SKr 3, over the tax payable abroad, SKr 0.5). Thus the risk is not merely that interest income otherwise taxable in Sweden will escape tax, but that revenues in Sweden will be further undermined by residents borrowing, and taking tax deductions, to acquire interest income untaxed in Sweden. The likely extent of such transactions is hard to judge, being in principle limited only by imperfections in the capital market. Certainly the attractions of such arbitrage are limited by spreads between borrowing and lending rates, and by exchange rate risk; but the former will become less of a concern as the efficiency of the banking sector improves (as stressed by Andersson and Fall, 2000), while the latter would be reduced if Sweden were to adopt the euro. Alternatively, one could imagine multinational corporations or banks (of which Sweden has many) performing tax arbitrage operations in house, almost costlessly and without credit risk. There are, indeed, signs that taxpayers are adept at exploiting the potential value of interest deductions: net revenue from the taxation of interest income is already negative, with net taxable interest in 1998 of minus SKr 19 billion.

There is thus reason to suppose that pressures to reduce the rate of tax on capital income will intensify. As noted earlier, the current rate of 30 percent on interest and dividend income is not among the highest of the top marginal rates in the OECD—but neither is it among the lowest. For those with relatively small amounts of capital income, moreover, the flat rate of 30 percent under the Swedish dual income tax is likely to be higher than the rate they would pay in countries that apply a progressive tax to an aggregate of capital and labor income.

One difficulty that would arise in lowering the rate applied to capital income is that it would intensify the incentives that currently exist under the dual income tax to transform labor income (taxed at marginal rates of up to 55 percent) into capital income. Policing the borderline between the two types of income is especially difficult for small businesses, since employees can acquire equity stakes, for instance, and take part of their employment income as lightly taxed return on capital.[82] Thus reducing the flat rate of capital income

---

[82]These practices are circumscribed but not made impossible by Swedish corporate law, which explicitly forbids the issuance of stocks without proper compensation, and formal rules that force the declaration of excessive dividend income as wages.

tax would put pressure on current levels of labor income taxation, amplifying the effect on total revenues.

These downward pressures on the flat tax on capital income may be mitigated by a recent agreement, in principle, to improve international cooperation with a view to strengthening personal taxes on interest income. Member states of the EU agreed in 2000 to move towards a mutual routine sharing of information, enabling them to bring under taxation their residents' interest income arising elsewhere in the EU.[83] Much important detail remains to be resolved, however—not least in terms of negotiations with key nonmembers, a prerequisite for action by the member states. At a technical level, the proposal to exchange information routinely is innovative, and its effectiveness remains to be tested. Doubtless the mere knowledge that information is being exchanged will have a salutary effect on tax compliance, at least in the early years of the scheme. The more fundamental difficulty remains, however, that the agreement will leave open opportunities for tax evasion through nonparticipating countries.

While there remain many imponderables in assessing the outlook for revenues from the taxation of savings, there is a clear downside risk. This risk is perhaps even higher than with the corporation tax, and may be of the order of a few percentage points of current tax revenues.

Commodities

The increased ease of moving commodities across borders, both legally and illegally, makes high indirect taxes harder to sustain.[84] Cross-border movement of commodities into and out of Sweden has become easier in recent years, particularly with the easing of fiscal controls at frontiers in the context of the EU's single market program and the expansion of links with the countries of the former Soviet Union. This facilitates the arbitraging of indirect tax differentials across countries—both through relatively small-scale, legal, own-use purchases by individuals, and through organized smuggling—and so potentially exerts downward pressure on both tax rates and revenue. High excises on alcoholic drink and tobacco are likely to come under particular pressure. The incentive for "cross-border shopping"—using this term to cover a wide range of transactions, from legal purchases within traveler's allowances to illegal

---

[83]Austria, Belgium, and Luxembourg would be allowed instead to apply a nonresident withholding tax over a transitional period.

[84]For a review of issues and experience in international aspects of commodity taxation, see Keen (2002).

smuggling and diversion frauds[85]—depends on the extent of tax differentials between countries. Irrespective of differentials relative to other countries, moreover, high indirect taxes in themselves run the risk of inducing evasion activities, including through the smuggling of goods that have not been taxed in any jurisdiction and illicit domestic production. As can be seen from the comparative indirect tax rates for the EU countries shown in Table 18, Sweden has the highest excises of any EU country on wine and spirits. They are far higher, in particular, than in Denmark or Germany, both easily reached from Sweden. The tax differentials this implies are amplified, moreover, by the high rate of VAT in Sweden—equaled only by that in Denmark—which is applied to the excise-inclusive price. Cigarette taxes are not out of line with those in neighboring EU countries, though the prospect of more open borders with nearby EU accession countries does pose a risk. The VAT rate itself is also sufficiently in excess of that charged elsewhere, notably in Germany, to risk generating tax-induced shopping on a broad range of items.

While cross-border shopping appears to be sizable in Sweden, its impact on budgetary revenues seems to be limited.[86] Table 19 reports estimates of the excise revenue lost from cross-border shopping. About one-third of the spirits consumed in 1996–97, it is estimated, were either smuggled or illegally distilled. For cigarettes, it is estimated that about 159 million sticks were smuggled, for a revenue loss of SKr 0.25 billion; the SKr 0.9 billion in the table comes from applying the same loss per stick to an estimate of 540 million sticks—a considerable increase—smuggled more recently. For alcoholic drinks, the forgone excise revenue is SKr 2.2 billion, with the associated VAT loss estimated by the ministry of finance to be SKr 0.94 billion. The implied total loss on excisable commodities is a little over SKr 4 billion, or around 0.34 percent of general government revenue. Even adding a loss of around SKr 0.75 billion in relation to new cars, the estimate for the excise revenue loss from cross-border shopping remains well below ½ of 1 percent of general government revenues.

While the downward pressures on excise tax rates implied by cross-border shopping are already being felt and acted upon by Swedish policymakers, there is little doubt that these pressures will increase. In June 2001, the government announced a reduction in the excise on wine by nearly 20 percent. The derogation under which Sweden is allowed to limit the quantities of tax-paid goods that travelers may import expires in January 2003. It may also be

---

[85]These are frauds under which goods claimed to be for export, and so relieved of domestic tax, are in fact sold on the domestic market.

[86]Data underlying the analysis in this paragraph come mostly from National Tax Board (2000).

Table 18. Indirect Tax Rates in the EU, August 2002

				Excises		
	VAT[1]	Cigarettes[2]	Unleaded petrol[3]	Still wine[3]	Beer[4]	Distilled spirits[5]
Austria	20	72.3	.407	0	.021	10.00
Belgium	21	74.4	.494	.047	.017	16.61
Denmark	25	81.7	.539	.948–1.419	.036–.0361	36.89
Finland	22	75.6	.559–.567	2.355	.286[6]	50.46
France	19.6	75.4	.571–.621	0.34	.026[6]	14.50
Germany	16	72.5	.624–.639	0	.008	13.03
Greece	18	72.8	.296–.316	0	.011	9.08
Ireland	21	79.3	.402–.506	2.73	.199[6]	27.62
Italy	20	74.7	.542	0	.014	6.45
Luxembourg	15	67.7	.372	0	.008	10.41
Netherlands	19	74.1	.608	.059	.055–.251	15.04
Portugal	17	78.7	.479	0	.072–.202	8.36
Spain	16	72.0	.396–.427	0	.008	7.40
Sweden	**25**	**69.9**	**.475–.478**	**2.269**	**.172[6]**	**51.52**
United Kingdom	17.5	80.4	.742–.791	2.500	.194[6]	31.68

Source: EU Excise Duty Tables (July 2001).

[1]Standard rate.

[2]As percentage of price of most popular category.

[3]Euros per liter.

[4]Euros per liter per degree Plato of finished product. (The degree Plato is a measure of sugar content and hence alcohol potential of the unfermented liquor, or "wort" from which beer is made; 1 degree Plato corresponds roughly to 0.4 percent alcohol content by volume.)

[5]Euros per liter of pure alcohol.

[6]Euros per liter per degree of alcohol of finished product.

that the Internet will further facilitate cross-border movements, although business-to-consumer transactions (the only ones that properly give rise to a consumption tax liability) have remained relatively limited so far; and only about 3 percent of the VAT base relates to digitized products that pose the most novel tax problems associated with the Internet. Some protection against erosion is provided by the minimum indirect tax rates set by the EU, which in due course may also come to apply to Sweden's Baltic neighbors. However, the potential future revenue at risk is significant. The yield from the excises in 1999 was about SKr 82 billion. Most of this comes from energy taxes, which are likely to be relatively robust against cross-border shopping. Nevertheless, even ignoring the associated reduction in VAT payments, a loss of one-eighth of this would reduce general government revenues by about 0.8 percent. Still larger sums would be at stake if the high standard rate of the VAT itself were to come under strain.

Table 19. Estimated Excise Revenue Losses from Cross-Border Shopping
(SKr billions)

Cigarettes[1]	Petrol	Wine	Beer	Spirits
0.9	0.2	1.3	0.5	0.4

Source: Ministry of Finance; and National Tax Board.
[1]See text for derivation.

Labor

Labor mobility is potentially a concern—in terms of both its potential distortion by, and effect on, the welfare state—mainly at the two ends of the income distribution. The risk is that measures of redistribution may give rise to emigration by the better-off (with consequent loss of tax revenues and skills) and immigration at the bottom end (with consequent pressures on the welfare state in so far as migrants are net fiscal beneficiaries).

The prospect of outward movement of labor in response to the tax transfer system has been a concern for some years. Indeed, Pomp (1999, p. 87) argues that "The departure of Ingmar Bergman, Björn Borg, and Ingemar Stenmark has done more to focus Swedish attention on the enormous erosion of incentives than the writings of all the economists between Stockholm and Stanford." How significant a threat this is to the current welfare state, however, is far from clear.

The first place to which one naturally looks for fiscal distortions to labor is the discrepancy in average effective tax rates on labor income between Sweden and likely countries for emigration. Table 20 shows the average effective tax rates that a worker receiving the average production wage (first column) or 167 percent of that wage (second column) would face in the countries of the EU. The first figure in each cell shows the rate taking account of income tax, employee's social security contributions, and transfers. To take account of the reduction in real incomes brought about by indirect taxation, the figure in parentheses adjusts also for VAT at the standard rate of 25 percent. This will overstate the combined tax burden to the extent that part of consumption will be subject to VAT at a lower rate than the standard rate, and to the extent that some income is saved (although the latter effect averages to around zero over longer periods, because VAT will be paid on the future consumption financed by today's savings). The conclusion that emerges from the comparisons in this table is moderately reassuring: though clearly high, relative to a number of member states, the combined tax burden in Sweden is not out of line with those in the other countries of continental northern Europe.

Table 20. Average Effective Income Tax Rates for a Single Earner, 1998

	At Average Production Wage	At 167 Percent of Average Production Wage
Austria	28.6 (40.5)	35.0 (45.8)
Belgium	41.8 (51.9)	48.7 (57.6)
Denmark	43.4 (54.7)	50.4 (60.3)
Finland	35.4 (47.0)	42.6 (53.0)
France	27.3 (39.2)	30.7 (42.1)
Germany	42.1 (50.1)	47.5 (54.7)
Greece	18.3 (30.8)	23.3 (35.0)
Ireland	24.9 (37.9)	35.9 (47.0)
Italy	29.1 (40.9)	33.8 (44.8)
Luxembourg	24.6 (34.4)	33.9 (42.5)
Netherlands	34.4 (44.2)	38.9 (48.0)
Portugal	18.1 (30.0)	24.5 (35.5)
Spain	20.2 (31.2)	12.8 (24.8)
Sweden	34.4 (47.5)	42.0 (53.6)
United Kingdom	25.2 (36.3)	27.0 (37.9)
Average	29.9 (41.1)	35.1 (45.5)

Sources: OECD (2000); and authors' calculations.

Note: Figure in parentheses is the VAT-inclusive average effective rate, calculated as $(v + t)/(1 + v)$, where v is the standard rate of VAT and t the effective rate preceding the parentheses.

The migration decision is affected, however, by a range of measures not included in these calculations. Levels of gross pay are likely to be depressed, for instance, by the relatively high level of employers' social security contributions in Sweden and, at higher levels of pay, by the extensive wage compression. Comparing net pay across countries within occupational groups, Andersson (1995) reports substantially lower net wages in Sweden. He also emphasizes, however, that account needs to be taken of the consumption benefits from public expenditure enjoyed in the various countries, on which score Sweden looks attractive. Moreover, the migration decision is more complex than such comparisons allow. Individuals may exploit tax differentials of different kinds at different times in their life, earning and saving in low income tax countries—perhaps repatriating earnings to their families in the home country—and then retiring to countries with low consumption and wealth taxes. On balance, while there are significant avoidance opportunities under the wealth tax, as noted earlier, Sweden would seem in a fiscal sense relatively unattractive to the wealthy.

Outward migration of Swedes has not been high enough to become a serious concern. Emigration does not currently appear high or increasing, even within the common Nordic labor market. In the 1980s, for example, an average of only 0.1 percent of Swedes emigrated, far below corresponding figures for Germany and Norway. In 1999, total emigration was about 39,000, compared with a total population of 8.9 million. While it appears relatively commonplace for highly skilled workers in Swedish multinationals to spend time working abroad, return migration historically seems to be high.

Sweden has been quite receptive to inward migration, with immigrants exceeding emigrants by around 14,000 in 1999—around three times the figure for the early 1980s. Immigration policy has been marked by a receptiveness to asylum seekers and refugees. In 1998, about 5.6 percent of the population was foreign born, a higher proportion than in any other northern EU country. In recent years, a high proportion of these—around 70 percent—have been asylum seekers, a group with a high welfare dependency. There appears to be no assessment of the net fiscal cost from this, although survey evidence continues to show a relative lack of political concern among Swedes (Brücker and others, 2002).

Looking forward, the key issue is the likely extent and impact of inward migration associated with EU enlargement. One estimate is that ultimately 2–4 percent of the population of the potential accession countries may wish to migrate to the current members (Brücker and others, 2000). Since people from these countries account for a higher proportion of the population in Sweden (3 percent) than in any other EU member except Germany—which suggests potentially strong family and community links—Sweden may be a target destination for a significant number of these migrants. Moreover, during its presidency of the EU in the first half of 2001, Sweden committed itself to a more liberal immigration policy toward these countries than did other EU members.

Assessing the extent of the likely inflow with any precision is extremely difficult. The relative generosity of the tax transfer system may increase the attractiveness of Sweden as a destination, but the state of the labor market is also likely to be important. Continued rigidities may make it hard to absorb inflows, which in turn will have feedback effects on migrants' decisions that tend to reduce the inflows. The impact on public finances depends on the nature of the immigrants, and could even be beneficial. If, as seems likely, they are largely relatively young and relatively highly skilled, perhaps with a high propensity to return home after a period of good earnings, the impact may be to strengthen the public finances.

Spending Pressures

The prospect of strains on revenue would be less of a concern if there were also prospects of reduced spending pressures. Unfortunately, this is not the case.

Demography

Population aging set in earlier in Sweden than elsewhere, and firm action has been taken to deal with the pension implications. By the early 1990s, the old-age dependency ratio in Sweden was already at levels that other industrialized countries are projected to reach only in the coming years (Hagemann, 1995). This prompted a major reform of the pension system in 1999—described in Box 3—which included the introduction of an automatic stabilizing mechanism, placing it on a financially sustainable basis.

After 2010, however, significant further demographic pressures can be expected, including from nonpension age-related spending. Projections in the 2001 budget show a sharp increase in general government expenditure from 2010. Excluding interest payments, this is projected to be around 55 percent of GDP compared with the current 51 percent. This reflects rising pension payments and an increase in other age-related expenditures on health and social services for the expanding old-age cohorts. While the larger pension expenditures will be increasingly accommodated within the new pension arrangements, substantial fiscal pressure—perhaps in the order of 3 percentage points of GDP over the next 50 years—is likely to emerge on account of other age-related spending.

Local Government Spending and the Equalization System

Control of local government spending is key to controlling the overall level of public expenditure. Local government spending on health, education, social services, and other items, mentioned in Chapter 2, accounts for over 40 percent of general government expenditure. Although subject to a balanced budget rule, with expenditure ceilings applying only to central government, there is some risk that pressures on the level of spending at the central level may be deflected into an increase in local spending.

Current equalization arrangements limit the incentives that local authorities face to improve the quality of the services they provide or limit the tax rates they set. In an attempt to redistribute resources towards poorer localities, funds are reallocated horizontally between them, with each ultimately receiving an amount equal to the product of their populations and:

> (Own tax base) × (Own tax rate)
> + (Average tax base – Own base) × ("Corrected" average tax rate),

where the averaging is across all local authorities, tax bases are computed in per capita terms, and the corrected average rate is 95 percent of the average, with further adjustments reflecting the division of responsibilities between the

Box 3. Reform of the Swedish Pension System

At the start of 1999, Sweden implemented a radical reform of its old-age pension system in response to the expected sharp increase in the dependency ratio over the coming decades, placing it on a financially sustainable basis. The preexisting system was based on a national guaranteed minimum pension, a public defined-benefit pension financed on a pay-as-you-go (PAYG) basis, private pension insurance, and trade union or occupational pension schemes. The reform transferred responsibility for non-age-related pension payments (survivors' and disability pensions) to the central government. In compensation, the National Pension Fund made substantial transfers to central government, contributing to a substantial reduction in public debt. Public funds associated with pensions remaining after the transfers constituted the buffer funds: four large funds competing on an equal footing from 2001, and a smaller one with the objective of investing in small and medium-sized Swedish enterprises not listed on the Stockholm Stock Exchange.

The new system applies in full to those born after 1954[1] and comprises two tiers: the main components are a public PAYG pension scheme (income pension) with associated buffer funds, and a fully funded defined-contribution scheme (premium pension). The bulk of the 18.5 percent of pensionable income contribution, 16 percentage points, finances the PAYG scheme. The remaining 2.5 percent is channeled by the Premium Pension Authority, a government agency, to privately managed pension funds offering fully funded pension rights, chosen by the income earner. All pension funds are strictly regulated and supervised. The activities of the public funds are also the subject of annual government evaluations performed each spring and published on June 1.

The new pension system has an automatic "balancing mechanism" that ensures that the system remains able to meet its obligations with fixed contribution rates and benefit calculation rules. The balancing mechanism stipulates that the system's liability is indexed to the growth in average income so long as the present value of the system's revenues and assets, including the buffer funds, exceeds its liabilities; if it does not, indexation is lowered until long-term financial balance is reestablished, at which time the system reverts to the original indexation rule. Under current projections, this mechanism is unlikely to be brought into play.[2]

The pension reform has significant implications for financial markets. Initially, the foreign exchange market may have been most affected as a stock adjustment in public pension funds triggered by a relaxation of their foreign exchange exposure rules ran its course. A noticeable medium-term impact is likely on the equity and bond markets, where the various pension funds will play an increasingly important role. The private pension funds are likely to go through a round of consolidation triggered by rising competitive pressures that could substantially reduce their numbers.

---

[1]Pensions for people born before 1939 will be paid according to the old pension system, while a prorated mixture of the two systems will apply for those born between 1939 and 1954.

[2]For an account of the system by one of its architects, see Settergren (2001).

county council and municipalities in each county.[87] This structure has two adverse consequences on the incentives faced by local authorities, best seen by noting that, for an authority charging the average tax rate:[88]

- Short of attracting a net inflow of migrants—likely also to increase expenditure needs—there is little revenue to be gained by increasing the tax base through enhanced tax administration or improving the quality of public services and the effectiveness with which money is spent. This is because the direct revenue gain from an increase in the local tax base is offset by a reduction in the transfer received.

- A small increase in its own tax rate will always increase the revenue it receives, since the usual limit to increasing revenue by raising tax rates that is implied by the contraction of the tax base does not operate: from the perspective of the local authority, any such contraction is offset by an increase in the transfer it receives.

While local governments are not simply "leviathans" concerned only with maximizing their own tax revenue, the inducement to inefficient and excessive expenditures, consequent upon such full equalization, is clear.

Political Economy

The Swedish welfare state has been built upon—and, as the outcome of the 2002 parliamentary election confirms, continues to enjoy—a broad consensus of political support, reflecting both a widespread egalitarian sentiment (also reflected in Sweden's strong record of support for developing countries) and,

---

[87]Since 2001, the equalization scheme also ensures that, for all localities, growth in net income after equalization would be at least equal to the growth of the average per capita tax base.

[88]More formally, suppose that the per capita tax base of local government k is a function $B_k(\tau_k, g_k)$ of its own tax rate τ_k and the quality of its public services g_k. Then, ignoring for simplicity the correction of the average tax rate in the Swedish formula, its net revenue per capita is:

$$R_k = \tau_k B_k(\tau_k, g_k) + [\bar{B} - B_k(\tau_k, g_k)]\bar{\tau},$$

where a bar indicates an average over all localities. Differentiating, under the assumption that k is small and takes the decisions of all other localities as given, one finds:

$$\frac{\partial R_k}{\partial g_k} = (\tau_k - \bar{\tau}) \frac{\partial B_k}{\partial g_k} \quad \text{and} \quad \frac{\partial R_k}{\partial \tau_k} = (\tau_k - \bar{\tau}) \frac{\partial B_k}{\partial \tau_k} + B_k.$$

For the hypothetical "average" locality—one whose tax rate is at the average level—there is thus no revenue gain from an increase in the quality of spending, and there is an unambiguous gain in revenue from increasing the tax rate. Essentially the same problems arise under the Canadian equalization system, a detailed analysis being provided by Bird and Smart (1996).

doubtless, some degree of vested interests. The retrenchment of the 1990s also had broad social support: with a budget deficit of over 12 percent of GDP in 1993, the need for scaling back public expenditure became clear enough. In the present strong fiscal position, however, there will be pressure to reverse some of the past expenditure cuts. These found some reflection in the spring 2001 budget (in which, for instance, the ceiling on unemployment benefit receipts was increased). Such pressures may be compounded by a sense, among some commentators at least, that the reforms of the early 1990s compounded the recession that followed—inducing precautionary saving by the prospect of reduced social insurance—and that the gains from those reforms may not have been as spectacular as their more ardent advocates projected.

Increased pressure for redistribution might also be expected, and perhaps is already perceptible, from the rise in before-tax inequality over recent years. The Gini coefficient for the distribution of factor income—movement of which has commonly been glacial—has increased by around 15 percent over the past decade. Table 21 shows a significant increase in overall wage dispersion, especially between the upper and lower deciles. Many models would predict such an increase in before-tax inequality to lead to increased political support for redistribution. Majority voting over a linear income tax, for instance, leads to more progressivity in the tax, the greater the amount by which the median income falls below the mean.[89]

The politics of redistribution[90] are complex, however, and there is some empirical evidence to suggest that higher before-tax inequality is associated with *less* redistribution. Persson (1995) suggests that this may be explained in terms of individuals' preferences being defined not only over their own consumption but also on their consumption relative to that of others. Taxation then serves in part to correct the external damage that each individual confers on others by working more. And, the more equal initial incomes are, the more this consideration may dominate over standard efficiency and redistribution concerns. When before-tax incomes are identical, for instance, all voters may agree on a high marginal tax rate in order to mitigate the mutual damage that each would cause others by earning more, but when incomes are dissimilar, the element of redistribution between them implied by progressive taxation may eliminate the consensus for such a tax structure. Another potential expla-

---

[89]The net payment to any household under such a scheme depends on the difference between its own income and the mean (the redistribution under such a scheme comes from the uniform subsidy component, the extent of which depends on the average income), and hence the net gain to the median voter is greater, the greater is this difference. See, for instance, Myles (1995).

[90]For a fairly recent survey of this rapidly growing area, see Boadway and Keen (2000).

Table 21. Wage Dispersion

	90/10 ratio[1]	50/10 ratio[2]
1992	1.69	1.21
1993	1.74	1.22
1994	1.78	1.23
1995	1.75	1.22
1996	1.79	1.23
1997	1.81	1.24
1998	1.90	1.26
1999	1.96	1.27

Source: Ministry of Finance.
[1]Ratio of wage rate of 9th decile to that of 10th decile.
[2]Ratio of wage rate of 5th decile to that of 10th decile.

nation is that of Peltzman (1980), who argues that a negative association between inequality and the extent of redistribution might be explained by a diminished sense of solidarity between middle and lower income groups as inequality increases. These issues are clearly complex, and relatively little understood. In terms of practical politics, however, there appears as yet no reason to expect a substantial erosion of intrinsic support for the present extensive government intervention in Sweden.

Changing Labor Market Institutions

Sweden's specialized labor market institutions have had a mixed record over the past decades. They have delivered stable periods with nearly full or fast-growing employment, as well as unstable ones characterized by rapidly rising unemployment. As noted in Chapter 4, Friberg and Uddén-Sonnegård (2001) distinguish three periods since 1970:

• The traditional centralized wage formation model, 1969–82. The key negotiating partners under the centralized framework were the Swedish Conferederation of Trade Unions (LO) and the Confederation of Swedish Employees (SAF), central organizations representing trade unions and employers, respectively. They sought to maintain full employment, but—relying on the safety valve of periodic large devaluations—ended up with a high wage-growth equilibrium characterized by annual nominal wage increases of over 10 percent.

• Decentralized wage formation, 1983–90. During this period, the emphasis shifted back and forth between central and branch or individual trade-union-level negotiations, still retaining the LO-SAF partnership. As a result, the wage determination framework moved toward a more decentralized, patently suboptimal, midpoint where social partners failed to internalize the macroeconomic implications of higher wage increases. This led to a price-wage spiral, with real wages increasing by only 1 percent a year on average during this period.

• Wage formation under stabilization policies, 1991–2000. This period commenced with a recession and soaring unemployment rates, convincing social partners of the need for restrained wage increases as part of a policy package to stabilize the economy. With a single hiccup in 1996–97, wage growth was halved to around 4 percent on average, as the Riksbank's inflation-targeting framework gained credibility and inflation expectations subsided.

Friberg and Uddén-Sonnegård concluded that, despite the widely varying outcomes, the wage determination process was largely unchanged since 1970: once inflation expectations and demand for labor were included among explanatory variables for wage developments, results of Chow tests indicated no significant structural break.

The bargaining framework has improved since the early 1990s but remains vulnerable to exogenous shocks. Two key lessons from the theoretical literature are that the middle ground between centralized and decentralized wage bargaining should be avoided (Calmfors and Driffill, 1988), and that some cushion is needed to avoid excessive wage scale compression (Flanagan, 1999). The approach evolving during the most recent period builds on these insights. It combines sound macroeconomic policies leading to low inflation expectations, a sufficiently strong centralized component to impose macroeconomic wage discipline, and enough elbow room for follow-up negotiations to reflect local supply and demand conditions within the macroeconomic constraints. The introduction of an agreed set of rules for bargaining, and the creation in 2000 of the National Mediation Office (to settle unresolved procedural disagreements without interfering in the wage determination process), provide useful additional safety valves. Moreover, the replacement rate provided by the unemployment benefit has reversed its increasing trend from the early 1990s, improving job-search incentives (Forslund and Kolm, 2000). While the bargaining framework, enhanced by these changes, performed well in the high-growth period through mid-2001, it has not yet been tested by adverse macroeconomic conditions and—as with all centralized wage setting regimes—remains highly vulnerable to sudden shocks. Much like a large ship, the Swedish labor market needs time to turn around if such shocks materialize, with painful losses dur-

Figure 23. Annual Hours Worked per Employee

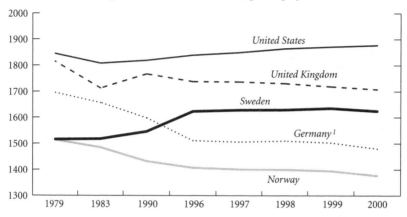

Source: OECD, *OECD Employment Outlook 2000* (Paris).
[1]Data from 1979 to 1990 are for western Germany.

ing the protracted adjustment process, as vividly demonstrated by the emergence of high unemployment in Sweden during 1993–98.

There may also be a need for the centralized bargaining framework to further adjust, even in the absence of shocks. With the working environment increasingly characterized by job rotation and multitasking rather than occupational specialization, the traditional centralized wage bargaining model becomes increasingly outdated.[91] The emerging new work organization is driven both by globalization and a shift in workers' preferences toward greater variation in work. It results in a flattening hierarchy of control and responsibility, more decentralized decision making, raises the demand for highly flexible labor with varied skills, and presupposes a finely nuanced incentive system. It is the last aspect that renders centralized wage bargaining highly inefficient in the new environment, since it continues to deliver uniform sectoral wages and a compressed wage scale. Such a wage structure cannot simultaneously support the high employment levels necessary for maintaining the welfare state and induce individual workers to perform the optimal mix of tasks that would allow firms to reap large benefits from the resulting complementarities.

As for the broader picture, various nonwage indicators also point to improving labor market performance during the past decade, but further

---

[91]See Lindbeck and Snower (2001).

Figure 24. Government Employment Index
(1970 = 100)

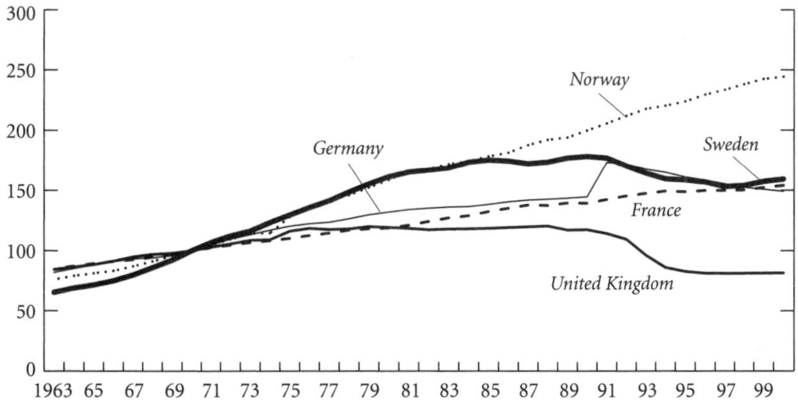

Source: OECD Analytical Database.

progress hinges on enhancing incentives to raise effective labor supply. Since the crisis period, the number of hours worked has steadily increased, and, with public sector employment curbed, most of the employment gains have occurred in the nongovernment sector (Figures 23 and 24). As noted in Chapter 5, however, absences from work have steadily risen since the mid-1990s, with a particularly worrisome increasing trend in sickness absences. While this level is not unprecedented in a historical perspective, and may in part reflect easing unemployment levels, the increasing trend is not sustainable. Considerable disincentive effects on the supply of highly skilled labor and on human capital creation may also stem from the still highly compressed after-tax wage scale. With the logic of the bargaining framework (whose stability requires a minimal wage drift) precluding substantial step increases in before-tax wage dispersion, tax policy measures are the only available instruments for rapidly bringing about a decompression of the after-tax wage scale.

Conclusions

The pressures that Sweden will face on the spending side in the years ahead are relatively clear. Those on the taxing side are harder to assess. It would be easy to exaggerate them: the constraints imposed by the international mobility of capital, goods, and labor are ones that Sweden has faced for some time. More generally, the surprising resilience of corporate tax revenues around the world indicates that the pressures on capital income tax revenues may not be as irresistible as has sometimes been thought. Nevertheless, the prospective forces at work all point in one direction: towards greater difficulty in raising tax revenue. Sweden, like others, is thus caught between upward pressures on spending and downward pressures on revenues. Estimating with any precision the severity of this tension is difficult, but might be on the order of a few percentage points of GDP—significant enough, in any event, to call for developing some strategy of response.

9 Achievements, Lessons, and the Way Ahead

This chapter takes stock of what Sweden's welfare state has delivered to its citizens, what others can learn from the Swedish experience—and which of these accomplishments can be maintained and furthered in the challenging years ahead.

The Quality of Life in Sweden

Even its sternest critics credit the Swedish welfare state with considerable achievements. As we have seen in earlier chapters, the average standard of living is high, as are equalities of income and opportunity; poverty, even on a relative measure, is low.

Not least, however—indeed perhaps most tellingly of all—Sweden ranks very highly in almost all indicators of the quality of human life. Sweden's public health, educational attainment, employment, and participation indicators are among the best in the world. According to Transparency International's 2001 *Global Corruption Report*,[92] Swedish business conditions are remarkably favorable: Sweden is the least likely place in the world where a bribe would be needed to retain business, and it ranks sixth—ahead of Switzerland, the United Kingdom, and the United States—in the ranking according to the Corruption Perceptions index. At 17 percent of GDP, genuine domestic savings[93]—savings corrected for resource depletion and human capital accumu-

---

[92]Transparency International (2001); available on the Internet at *http://www.globalcorruption report.org/#download*.

[93]Defined as gross domestic savings minus depreciation of physical capital, minus net depletion of minerals and energy, minus net depletion of forests, minus pollution damage, plus investment in human capital. See, for instance, Hamilton (1999).

lation—are significantly above the OECD average of 14 percent, and Sweden ranks fourth among all countries in the World Bank's environmental sustainability index. Development aid is among the most generous of all developed countries, and Sweden maintains an admirably open trade policy stance toward developing countries.

How much of all this can be attributed to government is unclear. But there is little doubt that—for all its imperfections and errors—government intervention has proved a help rather than a hindrance in pursuing a notion of social justice that has reflected a strong political consensus.

Lessons for Others

Sweden has long attracted special interest from policymakers and academics alike, being viewed as epitomizing an approach to economic life that sees considerable legitimacy for government to intervene in the pursuit of equity objectives while recognizing the importance of private incentives for the creation of wealth. The Swedish experience does indeed offer a host of lessons for other countries, concerning in particular:

- the design and development of a welfare state;

- preconditions for the survival of welfare states in the face of emerging pressures from globalization and demographic change; and

- its response to large shocks.

The Swedish model represents a social, political, and economic equilibrium that has been built over time and on a deep consensus. Many of its components—such as the extensive support system for human capital creation and maintenance, a transparent and efficient public sector to administer large-scale transfers and the provision of public services, and the achievement of high participation and employment rates—take a time to develop that is far longer than the normal political cycle, and require unwavering political support. Social cohesion underpinning the acceptance of a high tax burden has been essential to sustaining the Swedish welfare state. This cohesion in Sweden seems to derive not merely from altruism—though a substantial dose of this does seem to be present—but from self-interest too, as voters perceive potential if not actual benefit to themselves from measures of social insurance and redistribution.

These components of microeconomic policy have proved most successful in Sweden when complemented by sound macroeconomic policies, as in the past few years. A credible and stability-oriented monetary policy—such as that of the current inflation-targeting framework—has proved indispensable in preventing macroeconomic instability. Fiscal policy needs to be anchored in a sound medium-term fiscal framework, taking into account the underlying demographic developments, and committing the government to a sustainable path of spending and taxation while keeping public debt under control. Here, too, it may even be that interventionist policies have proved helpful. Some observers credit Sweden's generous family policy, for instance, with limiting the decline in fertility rates, alleviating the country's long-term demographic challenge: over the next 30 years, Sweden will go from having one of the highest old-age dependency ratios in the OECD to having one of the lowest.

Although public ownership and production remain high in Sweden, policy has long been marked by an awareness of the potential social value of preserving business incentives. Even when statutory corporate tax rates were very high, for example, relief was provided in a conscious attempt to preserve relatively low effective tax rates. More recently, high-tech activities have been allowed to flourish with a minimum of restriction or central direction. It might even be argued that the social insurance provided by the welfare state has itself encouraged risk taking, though we have seen that the evidence on this is, at best, unclear. Past experience seems to suggest, in any event, that further gains could have been realized from a more thorough commitment to the fostering of private enterprise.

At the core of the Swedish welfare state has been the raising and spending of a considerable proportion of GDP by the public sector. Earlier chapters reflected in some detail on the ways in which this has been done, and whether it might be done better. At a more general level, three features of the Swedish experience are of particular and wider interest. The first is that Sweden has long seen itself as a small open economy competing for internationally mobile capital and structured its tax policy correspondingly by offering relatively low statutory and effective tax rates. Globalization is in this sense nothing new for Sweden, though it seems likely that the quantitative implications will continue to become more marked. Other countries may be less well-prepared. Second, the focus of redistributive efforts has increasingly shifted from the taxing side of government activities to the spending side. This doubtless reflects the growing realization, in Sweden as elsewhere, of the potentially costly disincentive effects associated with high marginal tax rates. Especially striking, however, is the extent to which Sweden, and other Nordic countries adopting the dual income tax, have explicitly acknowledged the difficulty of taxing capital income. Despite the apparent popular appeal of the notion that capital income accrues mainly to the rich and so, on equity grounds, should be taxed at a relatively high rate, Swedish policymakers have managed to make the case that a less ambitious approach to taxing such income may ultimately prove more effective. Difficulties remain—revenue from interest taxation is still negative, though less so than before the 1991 reform—but the issue has been addressed in a coherent and thoughtful manner. Third, Sweden has relied extensively on universal benefits, having, in particular, no extensive means-tested in-work benefits of the kind that play a key role in, most notably, the United Kingdom and the United States. While this has meant a relatively high overall level of transfers, it has proved to be sustainable as a political equilibrium and may have helped mitigate marginal effective tax rates towards the lower end of the income distribution.

Sweden has also achieved considerable transparency and effectiveness in the management of its public finances. With a large public sector, such public trust and confidence in the government's stewardship is likely to be crucial in maintaining political support for extracting a comparatively large part of income to support redistribution. Given the considerable resources expended on public services, transparent and efficient public management is vital. Tax and benefit administration needs to be efficient to ensure a fair distribution of the tax burden, preserve confidence in the system, and limit disincentives by minimizing opportunities for evasion, abuse, and free riding.

The Swedish model also illustrates the potential value of decentralizing powers to lower-level governments, allotting them a critical role in the provision of many public services associated with the welfare state. In doing so, they are able to exploit their better knowledge of local circumstances and needs, and to do so in a framework that ensures political accountability. It is striking, too, that this is done with an allocation of tax powers quite different from the standard theoretical prescription. Textbooks generally prescribe that income tax be allocated to central government—for fear of tax competition between lower-level jurisdictions undoing attempts at redistribution (an analog of the fear at the national level discussed in Chapter 8)—and property taxes to lower-level government (because of the relative immobility of the associated tax base).[94] In Sweden, the allocation of powers is exactly the converse, and although this has occasionally been a matter for discussion, no strong pressures for reform have emerged. Why these arrangements have succeeded is not entirely clear; it may reflect in part the importance of redistribution on the spending rather than taxing side and consequent ability to mitigate incentive effects, and in part some relatively gentle but effective coordination at central level, for instance in terms of acceptable levels of social assistance.

---

[94]See, for example, Musgrave (1983).

Nevertheless, two cautionary lessons emerge from the Swedish experience of fiscal federalism. First, poorly designed regional revenue equalization schemes can have substantial adverse incentive effects. Second, efficient public provision of services need not involve their public production; a workable balance needs to be found, with private market participants providing public services wherever that allows a more efficient use of resources.

The institutions inherent to the Swedish model can complicate policy adjustments to large shocks. These shocks can come from either exogenous sources or from policy mistakes. In the worst constellation—as in Sweden during the early 1990s—these two kinds of shock can reinforce each other. If the shocks are sudden and large, rapid policy reaction is often crucial to minimize adjustment costs. In this case, however, the highly visible arrangements ensuring social peace (such as the wage bargaining framework), the rigidities associated with the large public sector, and the highly developed social safety net, all make rapid policy reaction harder. While they can be advantageous in tranquil times, such features can complicate the task of implementing drastic changes in policies. Thus, social cohesion was severely tested in the Swedish crisis of the early 1990s. While the system withstood the test, the institutional setting contributed—as discussed in Chapter 4—to the permanence of the adverse output effects.

The Swedish experience also points to the importance of recognizing and adapting in a timely fashion to secular trends acting slowly but with a potentially significant impact. The well-designed pension reform of the early 1990s is a case in point. Changes in market structure and technologies may also call for a reshaping of government intervention. Sweden has embraced technological developments in the telecom sector, in particular, to great effect. Less fully recognized in current policy, perhaps, are the ongoing and generalized shifts in work practices characterizing postindustrial, knowledge-based societies—the move away from occupational specialization to job rotation and multitasking—that may make the level of wage compression associated with centralized wage bargaining in Sweden unsustainable.[95] The relatively undifferentiated wage structure that centralized bargaining delivers can help maintain the high participation and employment rates necessary to sustain the Swedish model, but it is increasingly at odds with the need for individualized incentives for employees to engage in the multitasking, job rotation, and lifelong learning required by the modern workplace. Swedish experience also points to the potential cumulative adverse effects of a compressed wage scale on labor market flexibility.

---

[95]See Lindbeck and Snower (2001).

These lessons suggest that there is no reason, in principle, why the Swedish experience could not be emulated (or aspired to) in countries that have reached (or hope to reach) a high level of per capita income[96] and have a large degree of social commitment to the underlying notions of social justice and cohesion. But they reinforce the message that this requires strong political commitment, proficiency and clarity in policymaking, and a credible macro-economic framework. None of this is easy. Nor will it be easy for Sweden to deal with the problems that are now looming—many of which are also faced, in varying degrees and forms, by other countries.

Sweden: The Way Ahead

The Swedish welfare state is now at an important juncture. After the retrenchment of the 1990s, subsequent recovery, and now with a strong fiscal position, there are broadly two directions in which Sweden might move. One is to increase spending on transfers so as to restore some of the cutbacks of recent years. The other is to continue the streamlining of the 1990s, reducing the scale of government intervention by continuing to seek ways of improving incentives to work and save without jeopardizing core equity objectives, and focusing government activities ever more tightly on areas of market failure in which the government stands a good chance of doing better than the market. The analysis in this book, and the challenges that lie ahead for Sweden, lead us to argue for the latter strategy.

At its most basic, the key issue is the optimal size of government, which is in part an inescapable matter of ethical judgment. While there are circumstances in which equity gains can be achieved at no efficiency cost—as discussed in Chapter 6—once these have been realized, the issue ultimately boils down to trading off the efficiency costs of intervention against its equity benefits. Since value judgments come into play in assessing the latter, complete consensus on the proper extent of government intervention is highly unlikely: some may be willing to accept very high efficiency costs in return for modest improvements of the well-being of the worst-off; others may not. Moreover, although relatively well-defined conceptually, empirical and modeling issues leave considerable scope for disagreement as to the extent of the efficiency costs of the distortions associated with government intervention. Nevertheless, it is possible to derive some quantitative feel for the nature of the trade-

---

[96]Kornai (1997) characterized Hungary in the early years of transition as a "prematurely born welfare state" owing to the magnitude of transfers that could not be sustained at the country's level of per capita income.

off between efficiency and equity in Sweden and, hence, perhaps move toward some broad agreement on appropriate directions for change. An extremely stylized example of how this might be done is given in Box 4.

This exercise is no more than a very crude illustration, but taken in that spirit does suggest that at reasonable orders of magnitude—and even ignoring potential growth effects—the inefficiencies induced by intervention may plausibly be felt to exceed, at the margin, the equity gains. For example, suppose the marginal effectiveness of the tax transfer system in reducing inequality were equal to its average effectiveness, measured as the difference between the Gini coefficient measure of income inequality before and after taxes and transfers divided by the share of transfers in GDP. This implies that G'—the marginal reduction in the Gini coefficient associated with an expansion of government intervention—is about 1.5. (Since diminishing returns can reasonably be supposed to apply to inequality reduction, this is likely to be an overestimate.) Suppose, too, that the marginal excess burden of taxation (MEB)—the efficiency cost or raising an additional krona of revenue—is 0.75, corresponding (as discussed in Chapter 5) to the higher end of the estimates for a MELT of 60 percent. Then the calculation tabulated in Box 4 indicates that all observers who value a 1 percent increase in Gini-measured equality less than they do a 0.35 percent increase in average real incomes would wish to see the size of government reduced.

While the impact of extensive government intervention on the rate and quality of economic growth is hard to assess, easing the distortions to the incentives for working, investment, and saving could generate sizable cumulative efficiency gains. The illustrative figures for the marginal excess burden of taxation in Box 4 derive from a static framework. Though less extensively studied and understood, the cost of distortions that affect the long-term growth rate— part of which will be borne by generations yet unborn and so unable to directly represent their interest in current politics—could be even greater, reinforcing the case for tilting the balance to efficiency considerations.

But what clinches the case for renewed streamlining, in our view, is the prospect of significantly increased fiscal pressures. Though the extent of the effect is still to some degree imponderable, deepening internationalization will put continued pressure on the level and nature of government intervention. It will raise the efficiency costs of taxation, making it both harder and more costly to raise tax revenue—perhaps on the order of a few points of GDP. So too may changes in the pattern of collective bargaining. At the same time, the aging of the baby boomers will add to pressures from spending not only on pensions—this can be broadly accommodated within the reformed pension system—but also on other age-related items. We believe that the least painful

Box 4. Trading Off Efficiency and Equity

Suppose—very simplistically—that policy is evaluated by an objective function of the form $Y(T)[1 - G(T)]^{\alpha}$, where Y denotes average real income, G is the Gini coefficient measure of income inequality after all taxes and transfers, T is the total level of taxes and transfers, and α parameterizes the relative weight attached to average incomes and equality: a 1 percent increase in after-tax inequality is valued the same as an α percent increase in average real incomes. (The case in which $\alpha = 1$ corresponds to the Sen (1976) measure of real income.) The dependence of Y on T reflects the inefficiency cost of redistribution: normalizing Y to unity in the initial position, the derivative Y' is the negative of the additional excess burden of the system per dollar raised at the margin, MEB. Similarly the dependence of G on T reflects the impact of the system, on both the tax and transfer side, on after-tax inequality, the notion being that more intervention will tend to reduce inequality, so that the derivative G' is negative.

A small increase in T—the extent of government intervention—is desirable if and only if:

$$\alpha > -(1 - G)\,\frac{MEB}{G'}.$$

As one would expect, an increase in T is more likely to be desirable, for any given value judgment, the lower is the marginal excess burden it creates and the greater is the reduction G' in inequality it allows. More to the point, by specifying values for the MEB and G' one can infer from this equation the critical level of α—the weight one attaches to inequality—such that all those who care more or equally about inequality would welcome a further increase in the scale of intervention. Illustrative calculations are presented in the table below.

Critical Values of the Equality Preference Parameter α

$-G'$	MEB			
	0.10	0.50	0.75	1.00
0.5	0.14	0.71	1.06	1.40
1.0	0.07	0.35	0.53	0.71
1.5	0.05	0.24	0.35	0.47
2.0	0.04	0.18	0.26	0.35

Note: Initial inequality is assumed throughout to be 0.294 (the 1999 estimated value).

way of closing this incipient gap is likely to involve a reduction in the size of government.

Both on their own merits and to prepare for what may lie ahead, measures to streamline the role of government and focus on essentials should thus be continued and reinvigorated. Assessments of the 1991 tax reform and many other policy initiatives of the 1990s have been very positive. More can be done to better position the Swedish economy to preserve its considerable achievements. While forming a complete strategy requires addressing more questions of detail and undertaking deeper analysis than has been done in this book, some areas requiring attention are clear:

- The disincentive effects of high marginal effective tax rates on the better-off—a particularly productive group—could be reduced by cutting the top rate of central income tax and perhaps unifying the central rate somewhat below the current standard rate, all at relatively little revenue cost. By mitigating the problems that arise from the current disparity between the top rate of tax on labor income and that on capital income, this might also pave the way for an eventual cut in capital income taxation, which may well, in time, prove necessary.

- The more difficult problem of high marginal effective tax rates on the less well-off could be ameliorated by, for example, reducing the starting rate of the local income tax, or increasing the level of the child benefit and taxing it.

- High marginal effective tax rates on domestic savings could be eased, and the fairness of the tax system improved, by increasing the threshold for the wealth tax and tightening exemptions.

- Housing policy is characterized by a range of measures—de facto rent control, housing allowances, tax advantages to owner occupation—that have complex effects in a market that is key both to the efficiency of the labor market and the allocation of capital. A fundamental overhaul of these interventions, taking a holistic view of the interactions among them, is long overdue.

- Incentives under the sickness benefit scheme could be improved by having employers bear more of the cost, either by extending the period for which they are responsible for payment or by introducing some form of experience rating. More generally, the generosity of benefits—not only in terms of their levels but also the entitlement conditions attached to them—needs continual review.

- Further measures could be taken to alleviate the double taxation of dividends, which runs the risk of discouraging young and growing enterprises.

- Easing wage compression and other rigidities would improve labor market prospects for those earning lower wages (and ease the absorption of prospective immigrants as the EU expands), stem incipient emigration of high-skilled labor, strengthen incentives for human capital formation, and improve the allocation of labor across sectors and occupations.

- Ensuring a downward trend in the public expenditure share would safe-guard the authorities' medium-term surplus target.

Conclusions

Physicists have recently convinced themselves, it seems, that the bumblebee really can fly.[97] By the same token, it is hoped that this book will contribute to the understanding of the properties and nature of the economic, social, and political equilibrium that underlies the many achievements, and some of the weaknesses, of the Swedish welfare state. Both the bumblebee and the Swedish welfare state will doubtless continue to evolve. The latter, however, may need to do so more quickly.

---

[97]See Pennicott (2001); also available on the Internet as *http://physicsweb.org/article/news/5/10/9*.

Appendix   A Primer on Marginal and Average Effective Rates of Capital Income Taxation

This appendix develops the various effective tax concepts used in Chapter 6 to analyze the impact of the Swedish tax system on investment and savings decisions. This is an area of some complexity, both because of the wide variety of tax considerations that arise in modeling firms' financial and investment decisions and because of relatively minor but nevertheless awkward differences in the precise methodologies that various authors employ. The purpose here is to provide a relatively informal account of the basic concepts; more detail is provided in, for example, Jorgensen (1993) and Devereux and Griffith (2002). In particular, we do not consider here the precise ways in which taxation affects the cost of capital under alternative assumptions about the use of debt, retention, and new equity finance: see, for instance, the classic treatment in King and Fullerton (1984) or Mintz (1996).

The benchmark relative to which these concepts are defined is that of a world with no taxes, personal or corporate. Consider then a firm with increasing and strictly concave profit function $\Pi(K)$ defined on its capital stock K, and denote the interest rate by R and the relative price of the capital good by p. In the absence of tax, the cost of holding capital for one period consists of the real interest cost Rp of the money that is borrowed to finance or is otherwise tied up in the investment plus the true economic depreciation δp arising from the use of capital (reflecting both any change in its productivity and any capital gain or loss from the change in the relative price of capital). Thus the firm will choose K to maximize $\Pi(K) - (R + \delta)pK$, and so, as is well known, will set

$$\Pi'(K) = (R + \delta)p, \tag{A.1}$$

where the prime indicates differentiation.[1] The quantity to which the marginal product of capital is equated in equilibrium is known as the "user cost" (or

---

[1] While the discussion throughout is cast in terms of a single-period choice of the capital stock, essentially the same arguments hold in multiperiod contexts since the firm's optimization problem reduces to a series of single-period choice so long as there are no costs of adjusting the capital stock.

rental price) of capital; equation (A.1) shows that in the absence of tax this is simply $(R + \delta)pK$.

Now introduce corporate taxes. These may affect the before-tax earnings required to meet the costs of financing an investment in two main ways. The first is through the direct impact on financing costs. If an investment is financed by borrowing, for instance, then—assuming interest payments to be deductible against corporation tax—financing SKr 1 of interest payments requires only additional after-tax earnings of SKr $1 - \tau$, where τ denotes the rate of corporation tax. The second main effect is through the effective price of the capital good: with declining balance depreciation at a rate δ^T (quite possibly different from the "true" rate δ), the effective price falls from p to

$$p^T = p[1 - \{\tau\delta^T/[(1 - \tau)R + \delta^T]\}],$$

the difference between the two being the present value of the tax depreciation allowance (evaluated at the firm's discount rate, assuming debt finance, of $(1 - \tau)R$).[2] In this case, the profit-maximizing firm will set the marginal product of capital to:

$$(1 - \tau)\Pi'(K) = [R(1 - \tau) + \delta]p^T. \tag{A.2}$$

More generally—allowing for other kinds of finance than borrowing and for a range of depreciation schedules—the optimal capital stock is defined by the condition:

$$\Pi'(K) = C(T_c), \tag{A.3}$$

where T_c is the vector of corporate tax parameters (such as τ and δ^T).

The effects of the corporate tax system on the capital stock are then conveniently summarized by the difference between the user cost in the absence of the tax and that in its presence. It is this effect on the decision to invest that is captured by the marginal effective corporate tax rate (MECT), defined as:

$$MECT = \frac{C(T_c) - (R + \delta)p}{C(T_c)}. \tag{A.4}$$

By concavity of Π, the impact of the tax will be to reduce the capital stock if and only if MECT > 0. Note, in particular, that some corporate tax systems will be completely neutral, in the sense that they will leave the user cost of capital ex-

---

[2]This follows on noting that the present value of tax deductions is:

$$\int_0^\infty \delta^T e^{-\delta^T_s} e^{-(1-\tau)Rs} ds = \delta^T/[(1 - \tau)R + \delta^T].$$

actly the same as in the absence of tax. One such case—as mentioned in the text—is that in which interest is deductible and depreciation allowable at the "true" economic rate. In this case, it is easily verified, the right-hand side of equation (A.2) reduces to $(R + \delta)p$, exactly as in the right of equation (A.1). This is not the only neutral system, however. The same effect would be achieved by disallowing interest deduction but allowing all investment expenditures to be immediately deducted in calculating corporate tax liability. Indeed, there are many neutral corporate tax systems,[3] the key to neutrality being that, over the lifetime of an investment, all financial and depreciation costs—no more and no less—be deductible.

The MECT measures how much corporate tax will be collected on the marginal project that the firm finds to just break even: if the MECT is positive, the gross cost of the investment to the firm exceeds the final return to investors, so that positive tax revenue is collected. But tax will typically also be collected on *intra*marginal investments: ones, that is, which more than break even. This is clearest in the case of a neutral tax, for then the effect of the corporate tax is to leave marginal decisions unaffected but, at the same time, to capture for the government some of the rents on those unchanged investments. And for investors who can choose in which jurisdiction to locate an investment, the tax collected on intramarginal profits in each is clearly an important consideration.

The concept of the average effective corporate tax rate (AECT) is intended to capture the tax burden on intramarginal projects. To this end, note first that the after-tax profits of the firm are $V = (1 - \tau)[\Pi(K) - C(T_c)K]$: that is, life for the firm is as if it paid $C(T_c)$ on each unit of capital employed and then paid tax at the statutory rate on the profits it earned.[4] Before-tax profits are $V^* = \Pi(K) - RK$, so that the AECT is naturally defined as:

$$AECT \equiv \frac{V^* - V}{V^*}.$$ (A.5)

Recalling the definitions of V, V^*, and $C(T_c)$, this is neatly related to the statutory and marginal effective rates as:

$$AECT = \tau + \theta MECT$$ (A.6)

---

[3]Boadway and Bruce (1984) characterize a wide class of neutral schemes.

[4]To see this, suppose that the firm incurs costs AK, and can deduct an amount BK against tax, so that its maximand is $\Pi(K) - AK - \tau[\Pi(K) - BK]$. Optimizing over K, the user cost is then $C = (A - \tau B)/(1 - \tau)$; and the maximand can be seen to be simply $(1 - \tau)[\Pi(K) - CK]$. Essentially the same argument will hold in more general settings so long as the same kind of linearity in K holds.

where $\theta \equiv (1 - \tau)C(T_c)K/[\Pi(K) - RK]$ is the ratio of the net return on the marginal investment to the average before-tax return. This measure thus has the attractive feature that the effective average tax rate for a neutral corporate tax (one, that is, for which the MECT is zero) is exactly equal to the statutory rate, and exceeds the statutory rate if and only if the MECT is strictly positive.

A rather different definition of the average tax rate is developed by Devereux and Griffith (2002), and applied by the European Commission (2001). This takes output rather than rents in the denominator:

$$AECT' \equiv \frac{V^* - V}{\Pi}, \tag{A.7}$$

$$= \tau(1 - \lambda) + \lambda MECT, \tag{A.8}$$

where $\lambda \equiv C(T_c)K/\Pi$ denotes the ratio of the return of the marginal investment to the average return on the capital stock. Thus defined, the AECT does not have the desirable feature of coinciding with the statutory rate for any project under any neutral tax, but only for any neutral tax applied to a project with an infinitely high rate of return. It does have the advantage of being well defined even for projects with an average rate of return of zero; but this is easily accommodated by appropriate redefinition at this point, and the case is in any event a somewhat uninteresting one.

Suppose now that there are personal taxes, described by a parameter vector T_p, in addition to the corporation tax: T_p would include, for instance, the rates of tax on interest income, dividend income, and capital gains. In this case the user cost of capital will in general depend on personal taxes as well as corporate: the amount that a firm financing its investment by issuing new equity will need to earn in order to provide investors with an acceptable financial rate of return will depend, for instance, on the rate at which dividends are taxed. Thus equation (A.3) now becomes:

$$\Pi'(K) = C(T_c, T_p). \tag{A.9}$$

The net return required by the investor will now also be a function $S(T_p)$ of the personal tax system; if the investor's alternative is to invest at the market interest rate R with interest income taxed at the marginal rate m, for instance, then $S(T_p) = (1 - m)R$. The marginal effective personal savings tax rate, MEST— reflecting the wedge between the before-tax return on the underlying investment and the after-tax return to the investor—is then naturally defined as:[5]

---

[5]An alternative benchmark, focused more on neutrality, would be to replace S in (T_p) in equation (A.10) by the before-tax rate to the final investor, R. The $MEST'$ thus defined is simply that of the text less m.

$$MEST \equiv \frac{C(T_c, T_p) - S(T_p)}{C(T_c, T_p)},\tag{A.10}$$

It is this concept that underlies the estimates in Table 14 in Chapter 6.

As is evident from equation (A.10), the MEST in general depends on both personal and corporate tax parameters. It would be convenient if it could be decomposed somehow into effects arising from personal and corporate taxes in isolation. In general, however, this cannot be done. To see the difficulty,[6] note that MECT as defined above—and as generally calculated in the literature cited in the text—coincides with the MEST evaluated under the assumption of zero personal taxes: that is, $MECT = [C(T_c, 0) - S(0)]/ C(T_c, 0)$. From equation (A.10), one then has:

$$1 - MEST = (1 - MECT)(1 - MEPT'),\tag{A.11}$$

where

$$MEPT' = \frac{S(0)C(T_c, T_p) - S(T_p)C(T_c, 0)}{S(0)C(T_c, T_p)}.\tag{A.12}$$

Equation (A.12) is of the form one would seek in a decomposition into corporate and personal tax effects. But while MECT depends only on corporate tax effects, MEPT' in general depends not only on personal taxes but also on corporate. Only if the user cost of capital is unaffected by the personal tax system—not, in general, the case—is it possible to exactly decompose the overall marginal effective tax on savings into effects from personal and corporate taxes.

---

[6]This point is also addressed in King and Robson (1993).

Bibliography

Adema, W., 1997, "What Do Countries Really Spend on Social Policies? A Comparative Note," *OECD Economic Studies*, Vol. 1, No. 28, pp. 153–67.

Agell, Jonas, 1996, "Why Sweden's Welfare State Needed Reform," *Economic Journal*, Vol. 106 (November), pp. 1760–71.

———, 1998, "What Can the Welfare State Accomplish? An Introduction," *Swedish Economic Policy Review*, Vol. 5, No. 1, pp. 3–10.

———, L. Berg, and P.A. Edin, 1995, "The Swedish Boom to Bust Cycle: Tax Reform, Consumption, and Asset Structure," *Swedish Economic Policy Review*, Vol. 2, pp. 271–314.

Agell, Jonas, Peter Englund, and Jan Södersten, 1995, *Swedish Tax Policy in Theory and Practice: The 1991 Tax Reform* (Stockholm: Frizes).

———, 1998, *Incentives and Redistribution in the Welfare State: The Swedish Tax Reform* (Basingstoke: Macmillan).

Agell, Jonas, and P. Lundborg, 1999, "Survey Evidence on Wage Rigidity and Unemployment: Sweden in the 1990s," IFAU Working Paper 2 (Uppsala: Institute for Labor Market Policy Evaluation).

Aghion, Philippe, Eva Caroli, and Cecilia García-Peñalosa, 1999, "Inequality and Economic Growth: The Perspective of the New Growth Theories," *Journal of Economic Literature*, Vol. 37, pp. 1615–60.

Alesina, Alberto, 1992, "Political Instability and Economic Growth," NBER Working Paper 4173 (Cambridge, Massachusetts: National Bureau of Economic Research).

———, and Roberto Perotti, 1996, "Income Distribution, Political Instability, and Investment," *European Economic Review*, Vol. 40 (June), pp. 1203–28.

Alesina, Alberto, and Dani Rodrik, 1994, "Distributive Politics and Economic Growth," *The Quarterly Journal of Economics*, Vol. 109, Issue 2 (May), pp. 465–90.

Andersson, Kirster, 1995, *The Mobility of Capital—The Swedish Tax and Expenditure Structure in an Integrated Europe* (Stockholm: Ministry of Finance).

———, and Johan Fall, 2000, "The Ongoing Tax Competition in the EU to Attract Capital" (unpublished; Stockholm: Federation of Swedish Industries).

Apel, Mikael, and Jan Södersten, 1999, "Personal Taxation and Investment Incentives in a Small Open Economy," *International Tax and Public Finance*, Vol. 6, pp. 79–88.

Aronsson, Thomas, and James R. Walker, 1997, "The Effects of Sweden's Welfare State on Labor Supply Incentives," in *The Welfare State in Transition: Reforming the Swedish Model*, ed. by Richard B. Freeman, Robert Topel, and Birgitta Swedenborg (Chicago: University of Chicago Press).

Atkinson, Anthony B., 1995, "The Welfare State and Economic Performance," *National Tax Journal*, Vol. 48, pp. 171–98.

———, 1999, *The Economic Consequences of Rolling Back the Welfare State* (Cambridge, Massachusetts: MIT Press).

Balassa, Béla, 1978, "Exports and Economic Growth: Further Evidence," *Journal of Development Economics*, Vol. 5, pp. 181–89.

Banerjee, A.V., and A.F. Newman, 1993, "Occupational Choice and the Process of Development," *Journal of Political Economy*, Vol. 101, pp. 274–98.

Barro, Robert J., 1989, "A Cross-Country Study of Growth, Saving, and Government," NBER Working Paper 2855 (Cambridge, Massachusetts: National Bureau of Economic Research).

———, 1991, "Economic Growth in a Cross Section of Countries," *Quarterly Journal of Economics*, Vol. 106, pp. 407–43.

———, and Xavier Sala-i-Martin, 1995, *Economic Growth* (New York: McGraw-Hill).

Benabou, Roland, 1996, "Inequality and Growth," in *NBER Macroeconomics Annual*, Vol. 11, ed. by B.S. Bernanke and J. Rotemberg (Cambridge, Massachusetts: MIT Press).

Berndt, Ernst R., and Bengt Hansson, 1992, "Measuring the Contribution of Public Infrastructure Capital in Sweden," *Scandinavian Journal of Economics*, Vol. 94, pp. 151–68.

Bhagwati, Jagdish N., and T.N. Srinivasan, 1979, "Trade Policy and Development," in *International Economic Policy*, ed. by Rudiger Dornbusch and Jacob Frenkel (Baltimore: Johns Hopkins University Press).

Bird, Richard, and Michael Smart, 1996, "Federal Fiscal Arrangements in Canada: An Analysis of Incentives," *Proceedings of the National Tax Association* (Washington: National Tax Association), pp. 1–10.

Björklund, Anders, and Richard B. Freeman, 1997, "Generating Equality and Eliminating Poverty the Swedish Way," in *The Welfare State in Transition: Reforming the Swedish Model*, ed. by Richard B. Freeman, Robert Topel, and Birgitta Swedenborg (Chicago: University of Chicago Press).

Björklund, Anders, and Markus Jäntti, 1997, "Intergenerational Income Mobility in Sweden Compared to the United States," *American Economic Review*, Vol. 87, pp. 1009–18.

Björklund, Anders, Mårten Palme, and Ingemar Svensson, 1995, "Assessing the Effects of Swedish Tax and Benefit Reforms on Income Distribution Using Different Income Concepts," Tax Reform Evaluation Report 13 (Stockholm: National Institute of Economic Research, Economic Council, June).

Blackorby, Charles, and David Donaldson, 1988, "Cash Versus Kind, Self-Selection, and Efficient Transfers," *American Economic Review*, Vol. 78, No. 4, pp. 691–700.

Blanchard, Olivier, and Justin Wolfers, 1999, "The Role of Shocks and Institutions in the Rise of European Unemployment: The Aggregate Evidence," Harry Johnson Lecture (Cambridge, Massachusetts: MIT).

Blomqvist, Sören, Matias Eklöf, and Whitney Newey, 2001, "Tax Reform Evaluation Using Non-Parametric Methods: Sweden 1980–1991," *Journal of Public Economics*, Vol. 79, pp. 543–68.

Boadway, Robin, and Neil Bruce, 1984, "A General Proposition on the Design of a Neutral Business Tax," *Journal of Public Economics*, Vol. 24, pp. 231–39.

———, 1992, "Problems with Integrating Corporate and Personal Taxes in an Open Economy," *Journal of Public Economics*, Vol. 48, pp. 39–66.

Boadway, Robin, Katherine Cuff, and Maurice Marchand, 2000, "Optimal Income Taxation with Quasi-Linear Preferences Revisited," *Journal of Public Economic Theory*, Vol. 2, pp. 435–60.

Boadway, Robin, and Michael Keen, 2000, "Redistribution," in *Handbook of Income Distribution*, Vol. 1, ed. by Anthony Atkinson and François Bourguignon (Amsterdam: North-Holland).

———, 2002, "Theoretical Considerations in the Taxation of Capital Income and Financial Services: A Survey," in P. Honohan, ed., *The Taxation of Domestic Financial Intermediation* (Washington: World Bank).

Boeri, T., A. Börsch-Supan, and G. Tabellini, 2001, "Would You Like to Shrink the Welfare State? A Survey of European Citizens," *Economic Policy*, Vol. 16, No. 32 (April), pp. 7–50.

Boije, Robert, 2001, "Challenges for Tax Policy in Sweden," *Sveriges Riksbank Economic Review*, No. 2, pp. 50–79.

Bond, Stephen, and Lucy Chennells, 2000, "Corporate Income Taxes and Investment: A Comparative Study" (unpublished; London: Institute for Fiscal Studies).

Borensztein, Eduardo, Jose De Gregorio, and Jong-Wha Lee, 1994, "How Does Foreign Direct Investment Affect Economic Growth?" IMF Working Paper 94/110 (Washington: International Monetary Fund).

Brücker, Herbert, Gil S. Epstein, Barry McCormick, Gilles Saint-Paul, Alessandra Venturini, and Klaus Zimmermann, 2002, "Managing Migration in the European Welfare State," in *Immigration Policy and the Welfare System*, ed. by Tito Boeri, Gordon H. Henson, and Barry McCormick (Oxford: Oxford University Press), pp. 1–168.

Calmfors, Lars, and Mats Persson, 2000, "Economic Policy and Growth: An Introduction," *Swedish Economic Policy Review*, Vol. 7, No. 1, pp. 3–6.

Calmfors, Lars, Anders Forslung, and Maria Henström, 2001, "Does Active Labour Market Policy Work? Lessons from the Swedish Experiences" (unpublished; Stockholm: Department of Economics, Stockholm University).

Calmfors, Lars, and J. Driffill, 1988, "Bargaining Structure, Corporatism, and Macro-economic Performance," *Economic Policy,* Vol. 6 (April), pp. 13–61.

Carling, Kenneth, Bertil Holmlund, and Altin Vejsiu, 2001, "Do Benefit Cuts Boost Job Finding? Swedish Evidence from the 1990s," *Economic Journal,* Vol. 111, No. 474, pp. 766–90.

Castles, Francis G., and Steve Dowrick, 1990, "The Impact of Government Spending Levels on Medium-Term Economic Growth in the OECD, 1960–85," *Journal of Theoretical Politics,* Vol. 2, pp. 173–204.

Cerra, Valerie, and Sweta C. Saxena, 2000, "Alternative Methods of Estimating Potential Output and the Output Gap: An Application to Sweden," IMF Working Paper 00/59 (Washington: International Monetary Fund).

Chamley, Christophe, 1986, "Optimal Taxation of Capital Income in General Equilibrium with Infinite Lives," *Econometrica,* Vol. 54, pp. 607–22.

Chirinko, Robert, Stephen Fazzari, and Andrew Meyer, 1999, "How Responsive Is Business Capital Formation to Its User Cost? An Exploration Using Micro-Data," *Journal of Public Economics,* Vol. 74, pp. 53–80.

Cnossen, Sijbren, 2000, "Taxing Capital Income in Nordic Countries," in *Taxing Capital Income in the European Union: Issues and Options for Reform,* ed. by Sijbren Cnossen (Oxford: Oxford University Press), pp. 180–213.

Coe, David R., and Elhanan Helpman, 1993, "International R&D Spillovers," NBER Working Paper 4444 (Cambridge, Massachusetts: National Bureau of Economic Research).

Crafts, Nicholas, 2000, "Globalization and Growth in the Twentieth Century," IMF Working Paper 00/44 (Washington: International Monetary Fund).

Daveri, F., and G. Tabellini, 2000, "Unemployment, Growth, and Taxation in Industrial Countries," *Economic Policy,* Vol. 15, No. 30 (April), pp. 49–104.

Denison, Edward, 1967, *Why Growth Rates Differ: Post-War Experience in Nine Western Countries* (Washington: Brookings Institution).

Devereux, Michael, and Harold Freeman, 1995, "The Impact of Tax on Foreign Direct Investment: Empirical Evidence and Implications for Tax Integration Schemes," *International Tax and Public Finance,* Vol. 2, pp. 85–106.

Devereux, Michael, and Rachel Griffith, 2002, "Evaluating Tax Policy for Location Decisions," *International Tax and Public Finance* (forthcoming).

———, and Alexander Klemm, 2002, "Can International Tax Competition Explain Corporate Income Tax Reforms?" *Economic Policy* (forthcoming).

Diamond, John, 1989, "Government Expenditure and Economic Growth: An Empirical Investigation," IMF Working Paper 89/45 (Washington: International Monetary Fund).

Diamond, Peter, and James Mirrlees, 1971, "Optimal Taxation and Public Production, II: Tax Rules," *American Economic Review,* Vol. 61, pp. 261–78.

Doppelhofer, Gernot, Ronald Miller, and Xavier Sala-i-Martin, 2000, "Determinants of Long-Term Growth: A Bayesian Averaging of Classical Estimates (BAGE) Approach," NBER Working Paper 7750 (Cambridge, Massachusetts: National Bureau of Economic Research).

Dowrick, Steve, 1996, "Swedish Economic Performance and Swedish Economic Debate: A View From the Outside," *Economic Journal*, Vol. 106, pp. 1772–79.

———, and Duc-Tho Nguyen, 1989, "OECD Comparative Economic Growth 1950–85: Catch-Up and Convergence," *American Economic Review*, Vol. 79, pp. 1010–30.

Easterly, William R., and Sergio Rebelo, 1993, "Fiscal Policy and Economic Growth: An Empirical Investigation," *Journal of Monetary Economics*, Vol. 32, pp. 417–58.

Edwards, Jeremy, Michael Keen, and Matti Tuomala, 1994, "Income Tax, Commodity Taxes, and Public Good Provision: A Brief Guide," *Finanzarchiv*, Vol. 54, pp. 472–87.

Esping-Andersen, Gøsta, 1990, *The Three Worlds of Welfare Capitalism* (Cambridge, U.K.: Polity Press).

European Commission, 2001, *Company Taxation in the Internal Market* (Brussels: European Commission).

Feldstein, Martin S., and Charles Horioka, 1980, "Domestic Savings and International Capital Flows," *Economic Journal*, Vol. 90, pp. 314–29.

Flanagan, R.J., 1999, "Macroeconomic Performance and Collective Bargaining: An International Perspective," *Journal of Economic Literature*, Vol. 37 (September), pp. 1150–75.

Forslund, A., and A.S. Kolm, 2000, "Active Labor Market Policies and Real Wage Determination—Swedish Evidence," IFAU Working Paper 7 (Uppsala: Institute for Labor Market Policy Evaluation).

Freeman, Richard B., Robert Topel, and Birgitta Swedenborg, eds., 1997, *The Welfare State in Transition: Reforming the Swedish Model* (Chicago: University of Chicago Press).

Frenkel, Jacob, Assaf Razin, and Chi-Wa Yuen, 1996, *Fiscal Policies and Growth in the World Economy* (Cambridge, Massachusetts: MIT Press).

Friberg, Kent, and E. Uddén-Sonnegård, 2001, "Changed Wage Formation in a Changed Environment?" *Riksbank Economic Review*, pp. 42–69.

Fuest, Clemens, and Bernd Huber, 2000, "The Optimal Taxation at Dividends in a Small Open Economy," CESifo Working Paper Series, No. 348 (Munich, Germany: Center for Economic Studies and the Ifo Institute for Economic Research).

Gerson, Philip, 1998, "The Impact of Fiscal Policy Variables on Output Growth," IMF Working Paper 98/01 (Washington: International Monetary Fund).

Gottschalk, Peter, and Timothy M. Smeeding, 2000, "Empirical Evidence on Income Inequality in Industrialized Countries," in *Handbook of Income Distribution*,

Vol. 1, ed. by Anthony Atkinson and François Bourguignon (Amsterdam: North-Holland).

Griliches, Zvi, 1991, "The Search for R&D Spillovers," *Scandinavian Journal of Economics*, Vol. 94, pp. 29–47.

Gustafsson, Lennart, and Arne Svensson, 1999, "Public Sector Reform in Sweden" (Malmö: Liber Ekonomi).

Hagemann, Robert, 1995, "Social Security in Sweden," in *Challenges to the Swedish Welfare State*, ed. by D. Lachman and others, IMF Occasional Paper 130 (Washington: International Monetary Fund).

Hamilton, Kirk, 1999, "Genuine Savings Rates in Developing Countries," *World Bank Economic Review*, Vol. 13, pp. 333–56.

Hansson, Ingemar, 1987, "Marginal Cost of Public Funds for Different Tax Instruments and Government Expenditures," *Scandinavian Journal of Economics*, Vol. 86, pp. 115–31.

Hansson, Par, and Magnus Henrekson, 1994, "A New Framework for Testing the Effect of Government Spending on Growth and Productivity," *Public Choice*, Vol. 81, pp. 381–401.

Henreckson, Magnus, 1996, "Sweden's Relative Economic Performance: Lagging Behind or Staying on Top?" *Economic Journal*, Vol. 106, pp. 1747–59.

———, and Mats Persson, 2002, "The Effects of Sick Leave on Changes in the Sickness Insurance System," SSE/EFI Working Paper Series in Economics and Finance, No. 444 (Stockholm).

Hibbs, D.A., Jr., and Håkan Locking, 2000, "Wage Dispersion and Productive Efficiency: Evidence for Sweden," *Journal of Labor Economics*, Vol. 18, No. 4, pp. 755–82.

Hoff, Karla, and Andrew B. Lyon, 1995, "Nonleaky Buckets: Optimal Redistributive Taxation and Agency Costs," *Journal of Public Economics*, Vol. 58, pp. 365–90.

Holmlund, B., and A.S. Kolm, 1995, "Progressive Taxation, Wage Setting, and Unemployment: Theory and Swedish Evidence," *Swedish Economic Policy Review*, Vol. 2, pp. 423–60.

Ilmakunnas, Pekka, and Vesa Kanniainen, 2001, "Entrepreneurship, Economic Risks, and Risk Insurance in the Welfare State: Results with OECD Data, 1978–93," *German Economic Review*, Vol. 2, pp. 195–218.

Jäntti, Markus, and Sheldon Danziger, 2000, "Income Poverty in Advanced Countries," in *Handbook of Income Distribution*, Vol. 1, ed. by Anthony Atkinson and François Bourguignon (Amsterdam: North-Holland).

Johansson, P., and M. Palme, 1993, "The Effect of Economic Incentives on Worker Absenteeism: An Empirical Study Using Swedish Micro Data," *Journal of Public Economics*, Vol. 59, pp. 195–218.

Jorgensen, Dale W., 1993, "Introduction and Summary," in *Tax Reform and the Cost of Capital: An International Comparison*, ed. by Dale Jorgensen and Ralph Landau (Washington: Brookings Institution).

Kanniainen, Vesa, and Jan Södersten, 1994, "Costs of Monitoring and Corporate Taxation," *Journal of Public Economics*, Vol. 55, pp. 307–21.

Kay, John A., 1980, "The Deadweight Loss from a Tax System," *Journal of Public Economics*, Vol. 13, pp. 111–20.

Keen, Michael, 1999, "EMU and Tax Competition," prepared for the XI Villa Mondragone International Economic Seminar (Rome, July).

———, 2002, "Some International Issues in Commodity Taxation," *Swedish Economic Policy Review*, Vol. 9, pp. 11–45.

Kessler, Anke, Christoph Lülfesmann, and Gordon Myers, 2000, "Redistribution, Fiscal Competition, and the Politics of Economic Integration" (unpublished; Vancouver: Department of Economics, Simon Fraser University).

King, Mervyn, 1980, "Taxation and Savings," in *Public Policy and the Tax System*, ed. by Geoffrey Heal and Gordon Hughes (London: Allen & Unwin).

———, and Don Fullerton, eds., 1984, *The Taxation of Income from Capital: A Comparative Study of the United States, the United Kingdom, Sweden, and West Germany* (Chicago: University of Chicago Press).

King, Mervyn, and Mark Robson, 1993, "United Kingdom," in *Tax Reform and the Cost of Capital: An International Comparison*, ed. by Dale Jorgensen and Ralph Landau (Washington: Brookings Institution).

Kneller, Richard, Michael Bleaney, and Norman Gemmell, 1999, "Fiscal Policy and Growth: Evidence from OECD Countries," *Journal of Public Economics*, Vol. 74, pp. 171–90.

Knight, Malcolm, Norman Loayza, and Delano Villanueva, 1995, "The Peace Dividend: Military Spending Cuts and Economic Growth," IMF Working Paper 95/53 (Washington: International Monetary Fund).

Kornai, János, 1997, "Paying the Bill for Goulash Communism: Hungary Development and Macro Stabilization in a Macro Economy" in *Struggle and Hope: Essays on Stabilization and Reform in a Post-Socialist Economy*, ed. by János Kornai (Cheltenham, U.K., and Northampton, Massachusetts: Elgar).

Korpi, Walter, 1985, "Economic Growth and the Welfare System: Leaky Bucket or Irrigation System?" *European Sociological Review*, Vol. 1, pp. 97–118.

———, 1996, "Eurosclerosis and the Sclerosis of Objectivity: On the Role of Values Among Economic Policy Experts," *Economic Journal*, Vol. 106, pp. 1727–46.

Koskela, Erkki, and J. Vilmunen, 1996, "Tax Progression Is Good for Employment in Popular Models of Trade Union Behavior," *Labor Economics*, Vol. 3, pp. 65–80.

Krueger, Anne O., 1978, "*Foreign Trade Regimes and Economic Development: Liberalization Attempts and Consequences* (Cambridge, Massachusetts: Ballinger).

Lachman, Desmond, Adam Bennett, John H. Green, Robert Hagemann, and Ramana Ramaswamy, 1995, *Challenges to the Swedish Welfare State*, IMF Occasional Paper No. 130 (Washington: International Monetary Fund).

Landau, Daniel L., 1993, "The Economic Impact of Military Expenditures," World Bank Policy Research Department Working Paper Series, No. 1138 (Washington: World Bank).

Lee, Jong-Wha, 1994, "Capital Goods Imports and Long-Run Growth," NBER Working Paper 4725 (Cambridge, Massachusetts: National Bureau of Economic Research).

Lindbeck, Assar, 1993, *The Selected Essays of Assar Lindbeck*, Vol. 2, *The Welfare State* (Aldershot, U.K.: Edward Elgar).

————, 1997, "The Swedish Experiment," *Journal of Economic Literature*, Vol. 35, No. 3, pp. 1273–1319.

————, Per Molander, Torsten Persson, Olof Petersson, Agnar Sandmo, Birgitta Swedenborg, and Niels Thygesen, 1994, *Turning Sweden Around* (Cambridge, Massachusetts: MIT Press).

Lindbeck, Assar, and Dennis J. Snower, 2001, "Centralized Bargaining and Reorganized Work: Are They Compatible?" paper presented at the ECB Annual Labor Market Workshop, Frankfurt, Germany, December 10–11, 2001.

Lindquist, Matthew J., 2000, "Wage Compression and Welfare in Sweden," Working Paper 4 (Stockholm: Stockholm University, Department of Economics).

McCallum, John, and André Blais, 1987, "Government, Special Interest Groups, and Economic Growth," *Public Choice*, Vol. 54, pp. 3–18.

Maddison, Angus, 2001, "The World Economy: A Millennial Perspective," OECD Development Centre Studies (Paris: Organization for Economic Cooperation and Development).

Martin, Philippe, 2000, "A Quoi Servent les Politiques Régionales?" *Economie Internationale*, No. 81 (First Quarter), pp. 3–20.

Masson, Paul, 2000, "Fiscal Policy and Growth in the Context of European Integration," IMF Working Paper 00/133 (Washington: International Monetary Fund).

Mehrez, Gil, 2002, "Sick Leave in Sweden," in *Sweden: Selected Issues*, prepared by Axel Schimmelpfennig and Gil Mehrez, IMF Country Report 02/160 (Washington, August), pp. 39–44; available on the Internet at *http://www.imf.org/external/pubs/ft/scr/2002/cr02160.pdf*.

Mendoza, Enrique, Gian Maria Milesi-Ferretti, and Patrick Asea, 1997, "On the Ineffectiveness of Tax Policy in Altering Long-Run Growth: Harberger's Superneutrality Conjecture," *Journal of Public Economics*, Vol. 66, pp. 99–126.

Ministry of Finance, Sweden, 1995, *The Medium-Term Survey of the Swedish Economy* (Stockholm).

————, 2000, *Updated Swedish Convergence Program* (Stockholm).

Mintz, Jack, 1996, "The Corporation Tax," in *The Economics of Tax Policy*, ed. by Michael P. Devereux (Oxford: Oxford University Press).

Musgrave, Richard A., 1983, "Who Should Tax, Where, and What?" in *Tax Assignment in Federal Countries*, ed. by C.E. McLure, Jr. (Canberra: Australian National University), pp. 2–19.

Muten, Leif, 1995, "Sweden Considers New Corporate Income Tax Integration," *Tax Notes International*, October 9, p. 1591.

Myles, Gareth D., 1995, *Public Economics* (Cambridge, U.K.: Cambridge University Press).

National Tax Board (Riksskatteverket), 2000, *Tax Statistical Yearbook of Sweden 2000* (Stockholm).

Nielsen, Søren Bo, Pascalis Raimondos-Møller, and Guttolm Schjelderup, 1999, "Tax Spillovers Under Separate Accounting and Formula Apportionment" (unpublished; Copenhagen: Copenhagen Business School).

Nordhaus, William D., 2002, "The Health of Nations: The Contribution of Improved Health to Living Standards," NBER Working Paper 8818 (Cambridge, Massachusetts: National Bureau of Economic Research).

Nordström, Håkan, 1992, "Studies in Trade Policy and Economic Growth," Monograph 20 (Stockholm: Institute for International Economic Studies).

Olson, M., 1982, *The Rise and Decline of Nations* (New Haven: Yale University Press).

Organization for Economic Cooperation and Development (OECD), 1994, "Regional Characteristics Affecting Small Business Formation: A Cross-National Comparison," Working Papers (International), Vol. II, No. 8 (Paris: OECD).

———, 2000, "The Tax and Transfer System—Balancing Efficiency and Welfare," in *OECD Economic Surveys: Sweden* (Paris: OECD).

———, 2002, *2002 Annual Review—Sweden* (EC)/EDR(2002)10 (Paris: OECD, Economic and Development Review Committee).

———, annual, *Revenue Statistics of OECD Member Countries* (Paris: OECD).

Otani, Ichiro, and Delano Villanueva, 1990, "Long-Term Growth in Developing Countries and Its Determinants: An Empirical Analysis," *World Development*, Vol. 85, pp. 223–38.

Peltzman, S., 1980, "The Growth of Government," *Journal of Law and Economics*, Vol. 23, pp. 209–87.

Pennicott, Katie, ed., 2001, "Lasers Illuminate the Flight of the Bumblebee," *PhysicsWeb*, October 16 (Bristol, U.K.: IOP Publishing, Ltd.); available on the Internet at *http://physicsweb.org/article/news/5/10/9*.

Persson, Mats, 1995, "Why Are Taxes So High in Egalitarian Countries?" *Scandinavian Journal of Economics*, Vol. 97, pp. 569–621.

Persson, Torsten, and Guido Tabellini, 1991, "Is Inequality Harmful for Growth? Theory and Evidence," NBER Working Paper 3599 (Cambridge, Massachusetts: National Bureau of Economic Research).

———, 1994, "Is Inequality Harmful for Growth?" *American Economic Review*, Vol. 84, pp. 600–21.

Pomp, Richard D., 1999, "The State, the Individual, and the Taxation of Economic Migration," in *Income Taxation and International Mobility*, ed. by Jagdish Bhagwati and John D. Wilson (Cambridge, Massachusetts: MIT Press).

Romer, Paul M., 1989, "What Determines the Rate of Growth and Technological Change?" World Bank Policy, Planning, and Research Working Paper Series, No. 279 (Washington: World Bank).

Ruding Committee, 1992, "Report of the Committee of Independent Experts on Company Taxation" (Brussels: European Commission).

Sala-i-Martin, Xavier, 1992, "Public Welfare and Growth," Yale University Economic Growth Center Discussion Paper 666 (New Haven: Yale University).

Schimmelpfennig, Axel, 2002, "Fiscal Policy and Macroeconomic Stabilization in Sweden," in *Sweden: Selected Issues*, prepared by Axel Schimmelpfennig and Gil Mehrez, IMF Country Report 02/160 (Washington, August), pp. 3–38; available on the Internet at *http://www.imf.org/external/pubs/ft/scr/2002/cr02160.pdf*.

Schneider, Friedrich, and Dominik Enste, 2000, "Shadow Economies: Size, Causes, and Consequences," *Journal of Economic Literature*, Vol. 38 (March), pp. 77–114.

Seade, Jesus, 1977, "On the Shape of Optimal Income Tax Schedules," *Journal of Public Economics*, Vol. 7, pp. 203–35.

Sen, Amartya, 1976, "Real National Income," *Review of Economic Studies*, Vol. 43, pp. 19–39.

Settergren, Ole, 2001, "The Automatic Balance Mechanism of the Swedish Pension System" (unpublished; Stockholm: National Insurance Board of Sweden).

Sinn, Hans-Werner, 1995, "A Theory of the Welfare State," *Scandinavian Journal of Economics*, Vol. 97, pp. 495–526.

———, 2000, "The Threat to the German Welfare State," CESifo Working Paper 320 (Munich: Center for Economic Studies and the Ifo Institute for Economic Research).

———, 2002, "EU Enlargement and the Future of the Welfare State," *Scottish Journal of Political Economy*, Vol. 49, pp. 104–15.

Södersten, Jan, 1993, "Sweden," in *Tax Reform and the Cost of Capital: An International Comparison*, ed. by Dale Jorgensen and Ralph Landau (Washington: Brookings Institution).

Sørensen, Peter Birch, 1994, "From the Global Income Tax to the Dual Income Tax: Recent Tax Reforms in Nordic Countries," *International Tax and Public Finance*, Vol. 1, pp. 57–79.

———, 1995, "Changing Views of the Corporate Income Tax, *National Tax Journal*, Vol. 47, pp. 279–94.

Svallfors, Stefan, 2002, "Welfare Regimes and Welfare Opinion: A Comparison of Eight Western Countries," in *The European Welfare Mix: Institutional Configuration and Distributional Outcomes*, ed. by J. Vogel.

Tanzi, Vito, 1995, "Long-Run Growth and Public Policy," in *Social Capability and Long-Term Economic Growth*, ed. by Bon Ho Koo and Dwight H. Perkins (New York: St. Martin's), pp. 142–56.

———, 2000, "Globalization and the Future of Social Protection" IMF Working Paper 00/12 (Washington: International Monetary Fund).

———, and Ludger Schuknecht, 1995, "The Growth of Government and the Reform of the State in Industrial Countries," IMF Working Paper 95/130 (Washington: International Monetary Fund).

Tanzi, Vito, and Howell Zee, 1997, "Fiscal Policy and Long-Run Growth," *IMF Staff Papers*, Vol. 44 (June), pp. 179–209.

Temple, Jonathan, 1999, "The New Growth Evidence," *Journal of Economic Literature*, Vol. 37, pp. 112–56.

Transparency International, 2001, *Global Corruption Report 2001* (Berlin); available on the Internet at *http://www.globalcorruptionreport.org/#download*.

United Nations Development Program (UNDP), 2000, *Human Development Report 2000* (New York); available on the Internet at *http://www. undp.org/hdr2000*.

Wasylenko, Michael, 1991, "Empirical Evidence on Interregional Business Location and the Role of Fiscal Incentives in Economic Development," in *Industry and Location in Public Policy*, ed. by H.W. Herzog, Jr., and A.M. Schlottmann (Knoxville: University of Tennessee Press).

Weede, Erich, 1986, "Sectoral Reallocation, Distributional Coalitions, and the Welfare State as Determinants of Economic Growth Rates in Industrialized Democracies," *European Journal of Political Research*, Vol. 14, pp. 501–19.

———, 1991, "The Impact of State Power on Economic Growth Rates in OECD Countries," *Quality and Quantity*, Vol. 25, pp. 421–38.

World Health Organization, 2000, *World Health Report* (Geneva).

Index

Redistribution of income, 74–80, 97–98.
See also Transfers of income
Regional governments, 8
Rent control, 73
Rental price of capital, 113–114
Replacement rates, 55, 56
Research and development investment,
impact on growth performance, 39
Reverse causality, 42
Risk taking, impact of social insurance,
44–45
Ruding Committee, 85

SAF. *See* Confederation of Swedish
Employees
Savings. *See also* Investment
double taxation of dividends, 69–72
genuine domestic savings, 103–104
marginal effective personal savings tax
rates, 69–70
owner-occupied housing deductions,
72
property tax rates, 72
tax revenues and, 68–73
undeclared, 86
wealth tax and, 68, 69, 73
Self-employment grants, 60
Sickness absences, 55, 101
Sickness benefits, 11, 55–57, 79
Smuggling, 89
Social assistance, 11, 48, 77
Social care, financing responsibility, 8–9
Social democratic welfare states, 1n
Social insurance, impact on risk taking,
44–45
Social security
compensation scheme for employees'
contribution, 17n
impact on labor market incentives, 47
tax revenue contribution, 13, 17
Spirits, excise taxes, 89–91
Stabilization wage formation, 99
State of the World index, 39
State-owned enterprises, privatizing, 20
Statutory tax rate, 67–68, 84–85
Stock exchange, foreign ownership, 34
Stock options, 34

Student benefits, 79
Student loans, 11
Subnational governments, 8
Swedish Confederation of Trade Unions,
98–99
Swedish government. *See also*
Government expenditures
deficits, 4, 7
impact on growth performance, 37–39
labor market intervention, 47–57
revenues, 4, 5, 17–18
structure, 8, 19–20
Swedish model, 1–7, 17–20, 104–108
Swedish welfare state
achievements of, 2–3
advantages of, 3
changing labor market institutions
and, 98–101
economic costs of, 3, 4
features of, 1–2
future of, 108–112
impact of internationalization of
economic activity, 81–93
lessons for others, 104–108
political economy and, 96–98
quality of life contributions, 103–104
spending pressures, 93–96
support for, 2

Tax allowances, 65–66
Tax arbitrage, 87
Tax rates
average effective rates, 92
on capital income, 87–88
corporate taxes, 63, 64–68, 84–85
effects on per capita income growth,
41–42
income effect, 48–49
by income group, 58
indirect, 89–90
international comparisons, 14–15
marginal effective corporate tax rate,
64–67, 114–117
marginal effective labor income tax
rate, 49–53, 55, 57
marginal effective personal savings tax
rates, 69–70

The Authors

Subhash Thakur is an Advisor in the European I Department of the IMF. He holds a PhD in economics from the University of California, San Diego. He has worked extensively on European economic issues and published in the areas of international economics and macroeconomic policy. He has taught at the IMF Institute and the School of Advanced International Studies (SAIS) of the Johns Hopkins University.

Michael Keen is Chief of the Tax Policy Division in the Fiscal Affairs Department of the IMF, having been Professor of Economics at the University of Essex. He has published widely on the theory and practice of public finance, and is currently President-elect of the International Institute of Public Finance and Chair of the International Seminar in Public Economics. Founding co-editor of *International Tax and Public Finance*, he is also on the editorial boards of the *Journal of Public Economics*, *Fiscal Studies*, the *Economics of Governance*, and the *German Economic Review*.

Balázs Horváth is a Senior Economist in the IMF's European I Department. He worked mainly on transition economies and other middle-income countries before taking up the post of desk economist for Sweden in September 2000. He has published in the fields of econometrics, transition economics, and empirical studies on growth. He holds a doctorate from the University of Pennsylvania.

Valerie Cerra is an Economist in the IMF's European I Department. During her career at the IMF, she has worked on a range of developing and industrial economies, including other Nordic countries. Her research and publications focus on international economics and macroeconomics. She holds a doctorate from the University of Washington.